THE GRAND
Reunion

M.A. KAYE

ISBN 978-1-68197-935-9 (Paperback)
ISBN 978-1-68197-936-6 (Digital)

Christian Faith Publishing, Inc.
296 Chestnut Street
Meadville, PA 16335
www.christianfaithpublishing.com

Printed in the United States of America

I volunteered to go fight because I was bored with my life. I was looking for adventure. Also, I wanted to serve my country and kill the enemy. Even though I've only been at the front for a short time I'm surprised at how foolish I was in my haste to be a part of all of this. Nothing seems to make sense any more. I've realized I don't hate those people who are supposed to be my enemies. Wouldn't it be better if we cast our weapons aside and helped one another live a more productive life? I think the only one who benefits from war is the devil and his minions. We've allowed the talents of our entire generation to be wasted. I hope God forgives us when we stand before Him on judgment day.

> —From a journal found near the body of an unidentified soldier, November 10, 1918. He was naked, lying on the battlefield without any identification of individuality or nationality, known but to God.

I think heaven will be whatever we want it to be.

> —Anonymous soldier who died in The Great War . . . one of the millions and millions.

And God shall wipe away all tears from their eyes;
and there shall be no more death,
neither sorrow, nor crying,
neither shall there be any more pain;
for the former things are passed away. (Revelation 21:4)

1

The last somber tones of "Abide with Me" fleetingly rose to the heavens as family members tossed handfuls of sacred British soil onto the Union Jack-draped coffin of Private Thomas Sanderson Milton. At 111 years of age, the passing of the one-time lad from London completed the quiet transition of The Great War generation from their earthly existence to heavenly hosts.

As a boy, Sandy, as his family and friends affectionately called him, was imbued with the enthusiasm and nationalism of his times, and had happily rushed off to join in the celebration of war. Unusually large for his age, and lying about his true years of existence, Sandy was happily welcomed into the service of his nation. Along with many of his neighborhood pals, the cream of British youth and manhood, they marched off to the glorious tunes of "God Save the King" and "Rule Britannica," on their way to the training camps which would instill in them the pride and professionalism of being a soldier for the Empire on which the sun never set. Unlike large numbers of his generation, he had survived the horrors of the trenches and the great battles that had denied full lives and bright futures to millions who had so nobly put faith in the lies eschewed by their leaders, that it was glorious to fight and die for God and Country, or for God and the Kaiser, or God and the Czar.

He had spent the last years of his life in a state of physical deterioration, being lovingly wheeled to annual Armistice Day commemorations so people could witness the last living connection to the cataclysm which had changed the course of world history for the rest of days. Prior to his death, he hadn't spoken in years, suffering from the stroke which rendered him mute. No one knew that as he sat there, enduring the last decade of his life, unable to respond to well-wishers who shook his hand or acknowledge the words of those eminent orators who spoke with deep sincerity and reverence of the sacrifices of his generation, the emotional pain which racked his heart.

All of his thoughts in the last decade, especially since he lost the ability to communicate verbally, centered on the people of his youth. Riley, his older brother, his hero from childhood, died early in the war in 1914, not heroically in combat but from an accidental explosion during artillery training. Jack, his youngest brother, was killed in the great German offensive of 1918. Sandy had received word of his death hours before the fighting ceased at the eleventh hour of the eleventh month. For the next nine decades there was no joy which many thought victory in the Great War would bring forth. Life was more of an existence instead of an experience. In the solitude of his frustrating incapacitation, he pined away the days longing not just to see them, but to touch them once again.

Now that Sandy had passed, as quiet in the night as the star shells which had glittered over No Man's Land for four long years, The Great War had finally, and for real, ceased to exist. Even before his earthly remains were solemnly placed into the regal grounds of London Memorial Soldiers of the King Cemetery, the soul of Private Thomas Sanderson Milton of the British 1st Army of the British Expeditionary Force had already been welcomed through the gates of heaven.

With the blessing of St. Peter and a smiling nod from a welcoming God, the Grand Reunion had begun.

The Angels had known in advance when the celebration would begin, and they had spent the last few weeks of Sandy Milton's life on earth polishing the pearly gates to a high sheen in anticipation of an event heaven had not witnessed on such a scale since the August 2, 1956, earthly passing of Albert Woolson, the last soldier of the War between the States, which set off the grand reunion of the American Civil generation.

Hosts of heavenly angels were outfitted in new white silk and satin robes which symbolized the purity of God's paradise that they would be welcomed into to share with one another for eternity. Much to everyone's surprise, they would not be welcomed by a chorus of angels, but by a thousand choruses of angels. The voices of heaven, five hundred to a choir, had been rehearsing for months. God had always told them that he would tip them off to when the last person of this unique generation would fulfill his time on earth, and there would be plenty of time to prepare for a performance that would reverberate through the ages.

The millions of souls, blessed with the love of God and reincarnated back into their earthly bodies, were gathering from every region of heaven's sanctuary. The fresh faces of enthusiastic youth, the millions who had perished in the misguided folly of the early twentieth century, came forth to witness the welcoming of their last brother-in-arms into his eternal reward. They were followed by the others who had also died due to the collateral effects of the combatant armies. Endless droves of civilians, who had perished due to wayward shells and bullets, or from starvation due to the blockades the nations had place upon one another to starve the opposing warring nation into submission. Innocent victims, young and old alike, who had been executed in reprisals in the heat and brutality of war were alive again, smiles breaking across their faces as the realization that their deliverance day was upon them. Parents and kinfolk who had once grieved for the loss of their loved ones all the rest of the days of their lives, now wept more tears of joy than baptismal water the Jordan River could ever hope to hold within its banks. The sounds of cherubim and seraphim enhanced the occasion, and the emotions that surged through each person left them in a constant sensation of love.

As the gates of God's house were pushed open, Saint Peter led the procession of the most Holy Apostles to meet Sandy as he walked the last few yards up the golden path toward eternal life and happiness. He was no longer an old withered man who needed the use of a wheelchair to just sit erect. He was the young Sandy again, in the prime of his physical and mental prowess. He would now enjoy his life in a way he hadn't been able to while living in his human form. He could already see the results of the metamorphosis which had transfigured his body from earthly shell to heavenly entity. The transformation of his spirit and soul would now allow him to experience eternal life in all of its joyful expectations. It was what one had always thought it would be. No one would ever be old in spirit, and the best parts of life as one envisioned them were infinite.

The soft, sweet voices of a half million angels slowly melded into a symphony of beauty that was beyond human senses. It was as though an endless sea of roses were swaying in a constant gentle breeze, emitting an aroma that intoxicated one with the desire to just fall forth into them, and through the wonders of nature enjoy the beauty and warmth of God's embrace. All human apprehension exited the body, replaced by a spirit of unrelenting goodness and selfless love.

"Welcome to the House of the Lord," spoke St. Peter in the most gracious of ways to the last sheep of God's flock from the World War I generation. Fulfilling their ceremonial role, the apostles knelt down on both knees, hands folded, and prayed in unison.

"Our most gracious and loving Lord, please receive into thy kingdom Thomas Sanderson Milton."

The millions watched in reverent silence.

Sandy wasn't sure what to do, but that conundrum solved itself momentarily.

Quietly, the Lord appeared in front of him. Sandy hadn't seen him come from any particular direction nor heard any cheering or crowd reaction to let him know that He was coming toward him, but the reality was, he was now in the presence of God.

Their eyes met and Sandy could feel any vestige of evil that might still occupy his being exit him. The few dust-like particles that emitted from him vaporized instantaneously. God placed His hands upon Sandy's shoulders. Sandy started to bend his knees in an attempt to genuflect, but the Lord's hands gently prevented him from even making it to a curtsy. Their eyes never broke from one another's vision.

Thus spoke the Lord.

"Welcome home my child." His voice resonated in the ears of everyone present, though it was spoken to him so softly that Sandy thought at first he was the only one who could hear the words of his Savior.

God turned to the multitudes and spoke again.

"This is truly a wonderful day, let us all rejoice and be glad! The joys of heaven are yours to embrace, now is not just the time of your life, but the start of eternal life."

Amid cheers mixed with huzzahs and bravos which thundered through the divine setting, God silently removed himself from their presence. The mighty choirs of angels would continue to provide a melodic backdrop to the great celebration that now ensued.

As was everyone's experience in their first moments of entering heaven, Sandy stood in sheer and true shock and awe, trying to comprehend everything at once, which is not the way of the Lord. It would take time for him to fully comprehend an event like this which was happening on such an enormous scale. He was giddy with smiles and laughter as the realization made itself very clear to him, that somewhere amid the Grand Reunion were his brothers and family. It might take him time to find them among the mass of the World War I generation, but since this was heaven, he knew that all of his thoughts and dreams would be fulfilled.

2

The sounds of joy that continued to vibrate through the fresh heavenly atmosphere made it difficult at times for one to hear when another person was directly addressing them. To say it was crowded would be trivial at best. One cannot convey a full understanding to the reader, an earthly mortal, the reality of an entire generation coming together in the House of the Lord, to celebrate eternal life with family and friends once thought lost forever.

In the following encounter, it was the simple power of touch which reunited the souls of long ago, in a moment as tender as the day life slipped away from him. Death claimed him as he lay on the bloody and soiled cot in the makeshift hospital, which in reality was a century-old, shell-holed Belgium barn a few miles from the front lines where Lucifer's minions were snuffing out the lives of thousands of young men during the Battle of Passchendaele in 1917.

The gentle laying of her fingers in the palm of his hand ignited his senses. They were soft and felt like silk. They were caring and imbued passion.

His eyes lit up like a child trying to take in all of the presents encountered at first sight on Christmas morning.

"Jennifer," was all he could softly mouth as the joy and warmth of endless love coursed through his body. His body tingled from inside out.

Her gaze conveyed mutual emotions, as well as the tightening of her grip on his hand with both of hers.

"It's really me, Andrew. I told you before you passed that we would meet again on the other side." Her cherub smile shone through the lucid tears which slipped down her cheeks. Still speechless, he wrapped his arms around her and held her tight. The sensations that filled their senses made those experienced the one and only time they made love seem pale.

They had met a week before he died. Jennifer was a nurse on her first tour of duty. She was nineteen, as was he. They both still believed in the spirit of the war and had eagerly enlisted to serve Empire and King, and experience life beyond the confines of their island nation. Andrew had been sent to the hospital to pick up supplies for the company medic who was engaged in other responsibilities that particular day. He was angry in being made to feel insignificant by being sent for supplies. That was not the job of a frontline rifleman but his captain had taken a liking to the young boy and took it upon himself to try and save him from the inevitable fate most everyone on the front lines was due to experience, or at least put it off as long as possible.

They locked eyes the second he stomped through the flap opening of the hospital tent. She was in the midst of conducting inventory of supplies and dropped two rolls of clean white bandages upon first sight of him. She knew at that moment that he was her destiny, as he knew in kind that she was his. In the little time that the war afforded them after exchanging names and greetings of admiration, they agreed to meet later that night.

Andrew snuck away from his trench to be with her. Jennifer had a private tent with a soft blanket to lay on waiting for him when he fulfilled the rendezvous. They talked for hours in excited but hushed whispers, afraid they would give themselves away to some authority, but anxious to share all of their youthful thoughts and dreams with one another. They fulfilled their passion shortly before the sun rose, a new experience for both of them which would unite them forever. He made it back to his trench position before anyone realized he was gone, and in time to go over the top with one of the first waves of infantry whose job it would be to destroy the German machine gun nests which protected the enemy lines at the rate of six hundred bullets per minute.

The next time she saw him, he couldn't see her. They brought his broken body into the Belgian barn being used as a frontline emergency station. Haphazard trails of blood were smeared on her white apron-covered light blue dress from the dozens of shell-sliced and bullet-punctured young men who had preceded her Andrew into the once-serene structure of agricultural domesticity.

The stretcher bearers placed him directly in front of her, oblivious to the emotional connection shared between the angelic nurse and the physically wrecked warrior. Jenny's heart pulled inward in anguish when she recognized that the body in front of her, the one with the right kneecap blown off and shards of bone exposed to the world, and blood oozing from the right socket which was once occupied by an enchanting deep blue eye, with the left eye swollen shut, was her darling Andrew. She squelched her impulse to let out a gasp of horror by biting the backside of her bottom lip.

The red silk kerchief around his neck, now sopping up some of the blood which exuded forth from Andrew's sight-snatching wound, was Jenny's parting gift to him just a few hours earlier. She had asked him to carry it with him as a sign of her love for him and was surprised to see that he had actually tied it around his neck in such a way that the other soldiers must have surely seen it and most likely pointed their jocular barbs at him for being such a romanticist.

While a doctor began a cursory evaluation of his new patient, starting with the damaged knee, Jenny leaned close to Andrew and whispered as softly into his ear as she had when they were intimate earlier in the morn, "I am here to take care of you, darling. I will not leave you, my love."

She stayed with him all through the surgery which lasted hours, assisting the doctor in what both knew was a futile exercise. His leg was amputated at the knee and a specialist declared that he would remain sightless the rest of his short life. Other internal injuries created by concussions caused by the explosive force of hundred-pound shells had further beaten up his internal organs. Over the course of the next few days, an infection began to settle into his blood stream and he grew weaker by the hour. In every free minute afforded to her during that same period of time, Jenny sat next to him, holding his hand, calmly patting or stroking it, and quietly talking with him, sharing her plans with him of how wonderful married life with one another would be, especially with a brood of children that would make their lives full. He didn't say a word until a few moments before he slipped away.

"I love you always, Jenny."

His voice was soft, for with each utterance of each syllable his body reverberated with pain from within.

"I will see you on the other side, my love. I love you always, Andrew."

A few tears began to slide down the left side of Andrew's face, a miracle of sorts considering the damage that had been done to the surrounding socket. His last pulse of life was a feeble but enduring act of love as his fingers squeezed Jenny's hand. Through the mist of emotion created by her watering eyes, she kissed Andrew on the lips one last time before an orderly who had witnessed the last moments respectfully drew the white bed sheet up over Andrew's head before escorting Jenny away from the scene.

Now, home in heaven, he was beautiful once again. His piercing deep blue eyes soaked in Jenny's smile as they broke from their embrace. His leg was whole, giving him the strong set he had in his youth, before the war.

"I heard every word you said to me those last days," Andrew told her in a voice which reflected his admiration for her loyalty and love. "Your sweet words, and the soft strength of your hands as you held mine, they gave me the vigor to tell you what I did before I passed."

"And now," Jenny said, almost reverently without breaking eye contact, "we can marry like we planned. Imagine what kind of revelry there will be, and with all of our family members present, once we find everyone!"

They both leaned into one another and as their lips met they sealed their decision with a kiss that was as sweet as a freshly baked sugar-covered pie right out of the oven. Just the kind Jenny had talked about baking for him that majestic night they first spent together close to a century ago. Their time and tribulations on earth now behind them, they looked forward with undulating happiness to an eternity of joy and love.

Celebrations were taking place on all scales and in all manners. With the entrance of Sandy Milton into heaven, the souls of all those who had been waiting since their own demise were freed to rise up and enter through the gates of eternal life as well. No longer were they tethered to a grave, or their final resting place, whether it was on the bottom of the sea or buried under by mounds of earth due to a shell blast. Of all the ways that humans had deigned to inflict suffering upon one another prior to one's death, especially those which resulted in the destruction of the body in its human form, none could destroy the soul which gave it eternal life. In heaven, as befitting the miracle of life, the soul once again gave life to the reorganization of the human form as it was for each individual in the vision God had always intended for all members of His family.

Much as Jesus had cured the crippled and made the blind see while carrying out his ministry on Earth, his Father now endowed all those who entered into His home the attributes of mind and health that would allow them to enjoy their eternal life without flaws.

The only inconvenient issue that was encountered by everyone was the somewhat overcrowding that faced them in their search for loved ones and friends and whoever else one was looking for throughout the infinity of heaven. It was not overcrowding in the geographic sense, for space was never ending, and it appeared in all scenarios (as we will see portrayed throughout our narrative), but even in heaven one did not just appear out of nowhere, with the exception of God. Finally finding the person you were looking for might take a long time, but along the way, you might meet other folks who were a part of your human life as well. All of these scenarios would play out as The Grand Reunion would continue from its initial stages well into weeks and months, if one were to continue to measure time in heaven the way one used to do while living on Earth.

4

The hardy, one-time soldier from Belgium could see his wife and children standing together, hands locked, searching the crowds looking for him. The tears of joy cascaded down his face as they recognized his voice yelling for them to look in his direction. The last time he saw them was August 1914 in their home village of Battice as they were lined up and executed by soldiers of the advancing German army. He was in the back of a German truck, hands tied together and being prepared to be sent to a prisoner of war camp. The rumor which had spread and had frightened the Kaiser's Army so much was that civilian snipers, known as "franc-tireurs," were killing German soldiers after they had passed through a village already conquered from the Belgian army. To squash any future attacks by the franc-tireurs, the Germans were rounding up and executing up to ten civilians for every German soldier killed by the feared snipers. The brutal methods were enforced throughout many of the towns and villages of the small nation.

"Papa! Papa! Papa!" shouted six-year-old Emil and nine-year-old Marga as they jumped up and down, tugging on each of their mother's arms in the process. The stuffed teddy bear Emil was holding was flailing up and down as his excitement grew.

Clara Verhoven soon reversed the laws of motion, as she ran forward toward her husband and dragged the children along with her. They were the ones now being yanked at such a pace that their shorter legs barely touched the ground as they did their best to keep up with their excited mother.

Hugo wrapped his arms around all of them as they slammed into him. His grasp was such that he lifted all three of them off the ground as he hugged and kissed them with unabated passion.

"I pined for each of you every day of my life for sixty-two years," he managed to vocalize between forehead kisses and hugging, grunting sounds. "My precious Clara, my beautiful children, my family, I'm so sorry I didn't save you, I—"

While Emil and Marga clenched his waist, Clara stopped his oratory by locking her lips on his long enough for him to calm down and gain composure.

"You did nothing wrong, Hugo. It was the way life played out. You loved us every day until our last. You were a good father, and a wonderful husband."

Her words, through the silkiness of her voice, succeeded in soothing his frantic emotions. "We are here now," she continued. "Now we can enjoy raising our children, and . . ."

Even in the midst of all their frothing emotions, Clara had noticed two young men standing a few feet behind Hugo. They were indecisive in their behavior, seemingly trying to make eye contact with her while at the same time dropping their heads as if in shame or embarrassment.

She knew them.

Breaking her embrace from Hugo, but still holding his hand, she walked toward the duo.

Marga noticed who their mother was approaching and shouted, "Mommy, there are the soldiers!"

All of them soon stood clustered together, within arm's length of one another. A modicum of silence preceded their engagement.

"Neither of us knows what to say," offered the blond-haired youth who couldn't have been older than twenty years of age.

"We recognized your children first," suggested his friend, also sporting the same flaxen hair and late-stage adolescent facial features. "I remember the teddy bear toy he was holding in his hands when our officer ordered us to line everyone up." His words trailed off as he relived that hollow moment when the order to fire was given and their bullets cut down Clara, Emil, Marga, and seven other suspected franc-tireurs from the village of Battice.

"What are your names, boys?" asked Hugo. His voice harbored no anger or tone of accusation. It was asked in the same way that is used when two strangers bump into one another on the streetcar by accident and by some invisible mutual understanding, begin chatting it up with one another in the most friendly of ways.

"I am Johann Halder."

"I am Rudi Polder."

Both were barely audible in their formal introduction, still feeling the shame of their actions from the early days of the war. Simultaneously they offered themselves up to the mercy of the Verhovens.

"We are sorry for killing each of you," the words stumbled out. Turning to Mr. Verhoven, they also added, "We are sorry for killing your family, sir."

Hugo looked into their eyes and could see the remorse which he had seen every day he looked into his washroom mirror when he stood before it as he shaved. He too had killed during the war. In the days before he was taken prisoner he knew without doubt that he had shot and killed at least seven German soldiers. He knew that in the coming days he would be seeking out those soldiers and asking for their absolution as well.

Clasping both of their hands in his, uniting the three of them in a symbol of friendship, he spoke in the same tone he used when inquiring their identities.

"You are forgiven. You did as we all did when asked to serve our cause and our country. Judgment is not mine to make."

Clara approached them and gave each of the young men a kind peck on the cheek. Their weeping was broken by Marga's sweet voice of innocence. "Would you like to come home with us tonight to play games and have fun? We're going to have a lot of fun tonight because Daddy is back with us again."

Johann brushed his damp cheeks clear and knelt down in front of Marga. "I appreciate your offer, little one. However, we are now going forth to seek out our parents. It has been a long time since either of us has seen our father and mother as well."

In the midst of their celebration with their children, and in discussing the revelation that Johann and Rudi had made about their part in the demise of their children, Marga and Hugo had not considered the circumstances that followed the two remorseful soldiers after they moved onward from the events at Battice.

"Boys," Hugo called out to them since they had already started walking away from the Verhoevens. "Did either of you see your parents before the war ended?" he asked in a most gentle and serious tone.

"We were both killed two days after what we did in Battice," Rudi said with an apologetic tone.

"I bled to death after being shot in the stomach and Rudi was killed instantly by machine gun fire while trying to dress my wound as I lay on the battlefield," interjected Johann.

Hugo stood there in silence as he tightened his grip around Marga's shoulder and pulled her closer to his frame. He had never considered the fate of the men who carried out the crime against his family during the war. They had suffered also, as well as the parents and families of the young men who were doing their duty as part of a political and military machine that was bigger than them and had taken away their freedom to be just in their decisions. It was the first time Hugo had felt empathy for his enemies.

"Please," he said with a genuine loving tone, "come and visit with us after you have reunited with your families. My family and I would find great satisfaction in all of us becoming friends."

The young men nodded in agreement, and for the first time since their encounter with the Verhoevens, smiles emitted forth from their once-forlorn looking faces. They now beamed like rays of sunshine, their hearts and souls having been blessed by the power of true reconciliation. They continued on their way seeking their relatives amid the millions.

5

The monument was made of marble. Its size was decisive enough for everyone to see it a far distance away so that they could read the words that were emblazoned on it in solid gold lettering. There were no images carved into it, allowing the words that had been shaped by their author to once again sear their emotions into the hearts and minds of everyone who took in its words. It read:

"For the Fallen"
by Robert Laurence Binyon

With proud thanksgiving, a mother for her children,
England mourns for her dead across the seas.
Flesh of her flesh they were, spirit of her spirit,
Fall in the cause of the free.

Solemn the drums thrill; Death august and royal
Sings sorrow up into immortal spheres.
There is music in the midst of desolation
And a glory that shines upon our tears.

They went with songs to the battle, they were young,
Straight of limb, true of eye, steady and aglow.
They were staunch to the end against odds uncounted,
They fell with their faces to the foe.

They shall not grow old, as we that are left grow old:
Age shall not weary them, nor the years condemn.
At the going down of the sun and in the morning
We will remember them.

They mingle not with their laughing comrades again;
They sit no more at familiar tables of home;
They have no lot in our labour of the day-time;
They sleep beyond England's foam.

But where our desires are and our hopes profound,
Felt as a well-spring that is hidden from sight,
To the innermost heart of their own land they are known
As the stars are known to the Night;

As the stars that shall be bright when we are dust,
Moving in marches upon the heavenly plain,
As the stars that are starry in the time of our darkness,
To the end, to the end, they remain.

Despite the emotions people were experiencing with entering heaven and focusing on finding loved ones who they had not seen in more than a lifetime, they took the time to solemnly read the words once again by the poet who himself passed away in 1943 in the midst of the second great conflagration of the twentieth century. Many let their eyes read for them while others quietly spoke the words of great emotion, their lips slowly moving to the rhythm of the literary masterpiece.

They moved onward after recalling the words that summed up their generation's existence. The poem was written in September 1914, shortly after the beginning of The Great War and the casualty lists from the Battle of Mons were starting to make their emotional impact felt in the homes of thousands of families throughout England.

On a bench situated along one of the paths that crossed in front of the monument sat a middle-aged man who was more focused on watching the people who stopped to read the poem before moving on than he was with reading the poem.

"May we share some of the bench with you?" asked a young man in his early twenties. He was accompanied by a younger girl who appeared to be in her early teens as well as what logically seemed to be the parents of the duo. Seeing there wasn't enough room for all of them to sit he jumped up without hesitation and offered his place to the older woman and her daughter.

"Please, please. Have a place to relax."

The mother and daughter sat down while the trio of males positioned themselves behind the bench. Binyon silently studied them while they quietly read the poem on the monument. His curiosity piqued, he casually asked out loud to none of them in particular, "Why do you think they memorialized *this* poem? I'm amazed at how many people I've seen stop to read it, and all of them showing such respect for it. It's as confusing for me as it's humbling."

He didn't realize his last words had given himself away as the author.

The young girl turned her head so as to make visual contact with him. "My brother standing next to you died at the Battle of Mons. So for my parents and myself, I guess this poem has special meaning, but it's more than that. I think the words are for all of us, the entire generation from the time period. The words seem to summarize how we all felt not just during the war but throughout the rest of our lives, surviving with so many loved ones having been taken from our lives."

"Your words were comforting to us," the father interjected. "We always believed this day would come as you stated it would in the last verse. It made the long days of sorrow and mourning somewhat more bearable."

"I lost a number of friends myself during the war," Binyon said respectfully. "When I wrote this early in the war they hadn't been killed yet but when I began to hear how horrendous that battle was I found myself feeling emptied of an enthusiasm for life."

The young boy, the former soldier, placed his hand on Binyon's arm. "In the years after the war, your words kept our memory alive.

Your words were read endless times throughout the world, anytime people gathered to remember us, to mourn for us, to embrace our memory. We have stayed young, those of us who died. People reading your words today, as they enter through the gates of heaven, are now reminded that our days of anguish are over. Your poem may mean more in heaven than it ever did on Earth."

The mother, who had her firstborn back, her beautiful daughter sitting side by side next to her, her husband with his hands softly cupping her shoulders as he stood behind her, smiled at Mr. Binyon. "Our days of mourning are over. Today is Easter for all of us."

6

The Holy Palms dining hall, one of countless thousands which dotted the celestial landscape, emitted aromas which contorted the senses. Fresh-baked pies of every persuasion wafted forth their magical ability to awaken long-dormant memories while allowing the palate to enjoy explosions of flavor which many had not experienced since the days preceding The Great War.

Jean and Jacques Brisbois sat at one of the small round wooden tables sharing slices of warm blueberry pie and a bottle of cold milk to wash it down with great satisfaction. The twin brothers had been killed within minutes of one another at the Battle of the Marne in 1914. They had gone forward side by side with an élan shared by the thousands of poilus who believed their love for France would be enough to protect them from Krupp cannons which the Prussians used on advancing infantry with great enthusiasm. They had spent their last moments prior to the attack sitting side by side calming one another with their memories of being home in the family kitchen enjoying their favorite dessert.

What they once dreamed about was no longer illusory.

"Have another slice, each of you," the kindhearted words of their slightly gray-haired grandmother encouraged them as she poured each of them another glass of milk. Jean pulled the last piece of his first piece of pie off of his fork with his teeth and swirled the rich glaze and berry tang around his mouth while softly closing his eyes as he soaked in the sensuous experience.

Jacques finished swallowing a new gulp of milk that caressed his tongue and gullet with a soft and creamy texture that complimented the tartness of the blueberries and grandma's special homemade sweet butter crust.

Their grandmother smiled with content as she slipped a newly minted pie for her boys into the oven.

It was as though the war had never happened and the good life had never come to an end.

7

Outside of the Holy Palms where the Brisbois brothers were enjoying being home again, a young seventeen-year-old girl named Patricia Benton was slowly brushing her golden shoulder-length locks. Each stroke brought a sense of normality back to her life that had disappeared during the war years. No longer would she have to keep it cumbered up in a ball under a hairnet and a grimy wool hat.

She felt beautiful again.

Working on the production line making artillery shells had been a dirty job. It was ugly and demeaning. The chemicals one encountered while working turned her fingers an unhealthy shade of yellow, similar to that displayed by one suffering from jaundice. It sickened her heart to know that something she was helping to construct would be used to kill other human beings but she reconciled it with her conscience at the time by telling herself that it was her contribution to the war effort, and that by building more shells each day to help end the war as soon as possible, she was also contributing to the survival of her brother, Ryan, who at that time was serving at the front lines. To balance everything in her mind and make it all right, Patricia also spent the first hour after each shift at church praying, asking God for forgiveness for her part in helping to perpetuate the war for another day, an event that she always thought of as a crime against all humans.

Patricia never knew that Ryan did not survive the war.

Ryan never knew the Patricia did not survive the war.

Patricia's life ended early in 1917 when a tired coworker doing a double shift inexplicably lit up a cigarette that she smuggled into the work zone where they were handling highly flammable materials. The last thing Patricia saw was a flash of phosphorous that instantly blinded her exposed eyes, shortly before a resulting explosion blew her physical component into a hundred different shards of bone and skin. The remains of her and the seventeen other young women in her section were gathered and buried together in a community grave since it was impossible for authorities to piece together their separate entities. While the families had been informed of the deadly accident, the news had been censored from the public. The decision was based on the idea that deaths on the home front would be detrimental to the morale of the populace. Family members were informed not to write to their sons or husbands in the military about the incident as well, for the same reason regarding morale.

In a foul twist of irony, Ryan was killed a few days after Patricia's remains were returned to the earth when the Germans detonated a part of his trench during the Battle of Messines. Unknown to him or the other twenty-one men stationed with him, enemy sappers had succeeded in placing eight hundred pounds of explosives under their advanced outpost. The force of the reaction upon discharge buried most of the men in up to six feet of dirt and rocks. With the battle progressing, there was no time to retrieve their bodies and later once the fighting for the day waned, too many other concerns occupied the minds of the living in their own struggle for survival than digging for dead bodies that would just be reburied anyway. Like thousands of others from all nations, Corporal Ryan Benton would be listed as missing in action until the war ended.

"I bet up here they'll never make you bun your hair up or hide it under a net," Ryan said in a merry tone as he appeared in front of his dear baby sister. Patricia's smile and their immediate embrace was so ebullient that they bumped into others standing nearby as they rocked to and fro in each other's arms.

"Oh Ryan, you're as handsome as the day I last saw you in your dress uniform. It's been so long. I am so happy you are here. Have you seen Mum and Father? What was it like after the war when you got home?" The questions poured forth in a gush of excitement that did not allow Ryan sufficient time to reply to any of the inquiries. He kept her in his arms as they bounded back and forth. He waited for her adrenaline to subside so he could respond to her. As their emotions declined and became manageable, Ryan took a step back so as to see his sister's whole face and be able to directly converse with her.

"I never made it home, Trisha. I was buried under the earth when the Germans blew up my observation post. How come you don't remember what it was like at home when Mum and Father got word of my death?"

Her smile was in decline when she responded with great concern. "I was killed during the war when the factory exploded. That means Mum and Father lost us both in the war."

Their honor for their parents' feelings grasped at each of their hearts.

"Surely then it has been a century of great anticipation for this day," Ryan said calmly, short of showing despair. "Mum and Father must have spent the rest of their lives in mourning. It will be exciting to find them up here, and we can be together again."

Patricia pulled her brother close once again and whispered into his ear as they hugged. "We can't thoroughly enjoy this until we are all together. We will withhold our jubilation until we are with our dear parents once more."

"Agree," shouted Ryan. "Then let us continue to seek them out. I am sure we will find them soon."

They locked arms and set out on their search for their parents. It would not be a dangerous trek or one filled with great impediments or risks, but making their way through millions of souls all engaged in their own reunions with friends and loved ones, it would simply take a little more time. What made it easier to accept, as everyone here knew, was that their journey would only have a happy ending.

8

The mass of humanity made it difficult to find someone who one was actually looking for, but it was more strenuous for an individual looking for others he or she may not have known on a personal level. While living on Earth, John Allan Jarkovitz was an emotionally charged young man who took great devotion to the cause that was his life's calling. From his youngest days he had embraced the world of science and the desire to be a physician. He had found it fascinating that life could be held in his hands, and that he had the power to stop death in its attack upon the living. He was in college studying to be a surgeon when the United States declared war on Germany in April 1917. Like millions before him of all nationalities, the desire to be part of a great adventure was too much to pass up and he rushed off to enlist in the United States Army before the government had a chance to draft him.

Trained in infantry skills like every other draftee, John was then assigned to the medical corps, not as a surgeon but as a battlefield medic. The professional doctors and surgeons would be located in hospitals behind the front lines, but the medics would be involved in as much combat as the regular front line soldier, the only exception being that as a medic it was against the rules of warfare for him to carry a weapon. As a corpsman, John would seek out those on the battlefield who were casualties and dress their wounds as best as possible, giving them a chance to stay alive long enough to be removed from the area of conflict and transported back to one of the field hospitals for proper surgery and medical care. His baptism of fire came during the Battle of St. Mihiel in September 1918.

As the doughboys went over the top and moved forward from their trenches, the earth raised forth to meet them like giant claws. High-caliber German artillery shells erupted massive geysers of rock and soil across the terrain the young Americans traversed on their way to vanquish their foe. Within seconds of jumping off into the advance, John's ears were assaulted by a confused distortion of combined sounds. The shrill high pitch of incoming shells mixed with the curdled screams of pain being inflicted on the youthful Yankees who steadily proceeded into their earthly experience of hell.

John's senses twirled around his mind like a young child's toy top. His brain questioned his body whether it was logical to continue striding further into the destructive desolation awaiting him. His eyes tried to comprehend seeing body parts lying on the ground disassociated from their torsos. He could feel his heart pumping with so much adrenaline and fear that it felt like it was trying to bust out of its bodily enclosure. Perspiration saturated his once arid uniform.

His grasp on reality was returned to him courtesy of a land mine which was detonated by a colleague running a few feet ahead of him. Out of the corner of his eye he witnessed the lad being elevated into the air as if in slow motion as the earth pushed upward. A chunk of rock bounced off of John's tin helmet while the body of the new casualty blew into John's legs and brought him face to face with the earth. Lying next to the newly deceased, John noticed that both of the private's feet had been omitted from his body. His shins were shredded like tickertape and blood streamed forth from countless cuts. Death had been instant, and John was impotent to thwart its zeal.

Reality left him no time for contemplation. He saw the standing body in front of him buckle to its knees and fall forward as slimy body fluid splattered across the warm skin of John's sweat covered face and neck. John inched his way on his stomach to the anonymous casualty but could see before he reached him that the baseball sized hole in the soldier's back precluded him from offering any life saving aid to what was now a corpse.

Bullets ripped up spews of dirt in front of him. The Red Cross insignia on John's helmet and uniform sleeve did nothing to protect him from the callous inhumanity present on the field of conflict. Unarmed and only interested in offering aid to the wounded, he was as likely to become a casualty as those he sought to assist. He quickly crawled another few feet to his right to another comrade who was down but noted with just as much alacrity that he too was dead, multiple bullet wounds to the boy's face making him ugly in appearance to all but the mother who would be weeping her beautiful child's death upon notification by post a few weeks after his demise.

The intensity of the conflagration increased to the point that the sounds emitted by the next trio of men John witnessed in their final throes of life were muted. The decibel level established by the orchestra of shells, bullets, and bombs trumped those pitiful groans and gasps put forth by human lungs as they expelled their last breathes of life. Amidst it all, John continued to crawl along the ground with the intention of finding someone he could aide and provide comfort.

Reaching the rim of a newly minted shell hole, John peered in and for the first time encountered living wounded. He descended into its depths head first while simultaneously trying to triage the situation.

There were four of them. They were all lying on their backs against the forward slant of the shell hole. The farthest from him was holding his leg while trying to suppress his pain through a series of low grunts. The man next to him had blood on his face but John could see him blinking his eyes which meant he was conscious and alert. The third of the quartet was holding his stomach with one hand while trying to coax one last dribble of water from his obviously empty canteen which he shook to and fro over his open mouth. The last soldier was screaming in an almost hysteric way as he tried to staunch the flow of blood from his right wrist. The severed hand was lying on his lap.

"I'm here to help!" John yelled in a near futile attempt to project his voice over the continuing reverberations of war. In the security of the shell hole, John raised himself off the ground and moved to the sorry site that was the stomach wound. "I'll take care of you," he blurted out in unwarranted assurance as he opened his shoulder kit reaching for a rolled up bandage. As he pressed the unsoiled wrap against the profuse pool of blood seeping forth from the dying man's gut, their eyes met for a brief second.

John's eyes seemed to say to the almost deceased, "I don't know what to do for you," while the dying man's eyes seemed to say, "Thank you for trying." The act occurred with such brevity that he passed away in a shorter time than it takes the reader to review the event.

John took a deep breath in order to maintain his composure and turned toward the handless soldier. His shrieking had decreased to a whimper, one that said the pain had reached a point beyond hurting him anymore as well as saying that his body was shutting down. Blood still trickled forth between his clenched fingers that were trying to staunch the flow from where his hand used to be attached to his wrist. It was an act of futility.

John momentarily sized up the situation. The crippled soul presented his wounded arm to John in a meek manner. As John reached out to grasp it and dress it with a clean bandage the arm collapsed and its owner let out a struggled gasp, his last.

"Please help me," the tired voice pleaded, interrupting John's moment of dazed confusion. John turned toward the soldier with the blood smeared face.

"Where are you hit?" he asked. "I can't see your wound anywhere," he stated with frustration starting to emanate from his vocal chords.

The soldier rolled his eyes upward in apparent aggravation. How could this medic not figure out the source of his bleeding? His face was caked with it, and blood doesn't flow upward from a lower body wound. "It's under my helmet," he said with a certain deliberation.

John felt insignificant.

"Yes. I'm sorry," he whispered in embarrassment. John gently attempted to lift the heavy helmet off the suffering man's head but it wouldn't budge. It was as though the dry blood had sealed it in place. With the palm of his hand John pushed upward hitting the underside of the helmet. It popped off his head with a sound reminiscent of that of a soda pop cap being pried off of a bottle. Some of the looser blood which had pooled in his hair freely flowed down the man's face and mixed with the dry blood making his face a messy canvas of bright red and dry rouge. Some of it swished into the wounded man's eyes and he squinted in irritation.

"My arms are broke," he mumbled. "Wipe my eyes. Please."

John hurriedly took out his canteen and uncapped it. Overanxious, nervous, and filled with excitement, his intention to gently pour water into the man's eyes to clean them instead became a haphazard gusher of water that slapped into the wounded man's forehead. John swore at himself in anger.

"It's okay, buddy, you tried."

His head slumped forward, his chin finding a final resting place on his chest. Between matted blond hair, John could see multiple gashes and a small hole near the top of the late man's head. He noticed no dents or holes in the dead man's helmet and couldn't figure out the origins of the wounds. But there wasn't time to dwell on the mystery as he quickly turned toward the man who had, at first glance, the non-life-threatening leg injury.

"How's the leg, soldier?" he asked as he sidled up to him.

There was no response.

John looked at the man and realized he was dead. He was looking straight ahead. His eyes were wide open. His arms were at his sides.

John was dumbfounded. An anterior physical wound was nowhere to be visualized. With a rawness eating at his stomach, and a curiosity that had to be satiated, John pulled the body forward by the shoulders. A piece of jagged shrapnel protruded from the base of the neck and the life blood which escaped the body vessel had drained down his back. The side of the shell hole he had been leaning against was also discolored with his plasma.

John let go of the body and stumbled backward to the opposite side of the shell crater. His back slammed into the hardness of the earth and he found himself sitting there staring at the four dead men. He could feel a sense of hollowness filling up his body from within. The eerie sensation crawled up his legs like a slow-moving caterpillar and soon found its way into the lining of his stomach. It began to gnaw at him and his arms tingled amid the sweat that aerated through his pores. His mind became a jumble of deteriorating thoughts as the dry heaves evolved into a fluid and chunk-filled regurgitation of all that physically remained within him. The salty tears that flooded forth mixed with the mucous emitting from his nostrils and combined with the spittle that clung to his mouth and chin from the violent upheaval that had been experienced by his stomach.

When they found him in the aftermath of the battle, he was mentally unconscious. His eyes were wide open and they flittered back and forth silently reviewing the four dead soldiers across from him. He was oblivious to the odiferous aroma which his fouled uniform emitted as well as to the flies which had started to land on him with the intent to enjoy a feast only they could participate in with tasteful satisfaction.

The only times throughout the rest of his depressingly sad short life that John ever spoke were in his nightmares and when he awoke screaming from those nightmares. The shock and disillusionment made him a self-invoked mute who could just never find it in his desire or ability to vocalize about the events he experienced in just a little under one hour of his life on that one specific day. The physical horror he witnessed was surpassed by the intellectual destruction that took place within his mind within the confines of that shell hole. The spirit of humanity which had motivated him prior to the war was replaced by a dead spirit of reality as one by one those soldiers died before his hands.

As he walked amongst the throngs that populated the infinity of heaven, he kept his eyes peeled looking for the "Dead Four," as he had come to remember them in the silent chambers of his memory. The phrase was all his, never once vocalized to any of the countless physicians, psychologists, and psychiatrists who had attempted throughout the remainder of his earthly life to get him to divulge his inner pain to them. While he did not know their names, he knew he would recognize them when he saw them. He had seen each of their faces nightly as his subconscious forced him to relive their deaths and his failure to save them over and over again. What he couldn't speak about he tried to write about in his last letter.

"My heart wanted to save those boys, but my mind and my hands failed me. I pray God Almighty forgive me for my lack of action. I was, and am, useless."

The letter was found on the floor of his sanitarium room, a short distance from his dangling feet, his body suspended from a ceiling fan that struggled to rotate as the dead weight of his body pulled it a tad loose from its screws.

After hours of diligent searching and scanning of thousands of faces, John made his way to the periphery of the newly resurrected to find himself looking out over a vast expanse of land. It didn't take him long to realize that it was the battlefield of his self-believed failure in 1918. As he gingerly proceeded, sidestepping craters, discarded accouterments of war, and twisted remnants of trees, his heartbeat began to accelerate. Ahead was the shell hole. His feet raced on ahead faster than his thoughts could carry him.

He stopped atop of the rim and stared down, meeting their eyes in a wonder of joy that can't be fully explained. Their images blurred as tears invalidated his vision for a fleeting moment. They were there, sitting side by side, alive, smiling at him, their arms thrust forward toward him, their hands reaching out for him, encouraging him forward into their grasp.

John was so excited that he literally fell forward into the shell hole, only to be held up by their strong, youthful arms filled with the strength of life.

"They're not broken anymore, Doc," one of them said.

As their arms wrapped around him in great bear hugs, John could only sob. "I'm sorry I couldn't save you boys, I tried, I'm sorry, I thought about you every day of my life, I'm sorry . . ."

"It's okay, Doc," they all chimed in at various times.

"We knew you tried, Doc, and we know what you went through because of it," said the youngest of the group.

As John regained his composure, and they released their embraces of him, he took a step back to look at them, and soak in their appearances. They were so clean now, free of the grime of combat and battlefield wounds. Gone were the pasty dry and vibrant shades of blood which had added such discourse to their features that awful day. Their bodies were whole again, youthful and vibrant, strong and beautiful.

John smiled and then stuttered. "I've mourned all these years for each of you, and I'm so sorry I failed you, and I don't even know your names. I . . ."

"Doc, I'm Charles Bordeau," he said as he stepped forward to shake John's hand. "This good looking lad is my best friend, Philip A. Brooks."

"I'm Dimitrious Stratikopulos."

"And I'm Clifford Dimmitt."

He took a deep breath and quietly said with aplomb, "I am John Jarkovitz." His smile then faded. "But I don't think I'm much of a doctor, though I thank you men kindly for the respect you have shown me."

"You tried, Doc," Clifford interjected. "I was the last of us to die in the shell hole. While I was bleeding out with my head wound, I could still see what you tried to do for each of us. I was struck by your genuine concern for us. I never knew some stranger would emit such emotion trying to save four young kids from Iowa."

John was tearing up again and quickly brushed the moisture away with his sleeve. "I grew up a Quaker in Pennsylvania," he said sheepishly. "I just thought everybody was worth saving."

"We all appreciate that, Doc," said Dimitrious. "It goes to the heart of what kind of person you are. After you meet up with your family, bring them around and we'll share a meal together."

"I killed myself after the war," John offered solemnly. "I'm not sure why I'm here with you fine men."

"That might be easier for you to understand than you realize, Doc," Clifford said with authority in his voice. "You put us first, in the midst of great danger to yourself. The Good Book says whatever you do for the least of my brothers, you do for me. You put others first. Your love for your fellow man, and strangers at that, didn't go unnoticed . . . and this is your just reward."

9

A short distance away in what was called "The Meadow of Peace and Meditation," former belligerents sat side by side soaking in the calmness of silence. German gunners, who had rained down ninety-two-pound shells from their Krupp Field Howitzers by the thousands, relaxed shoulder to shoulder with British field gunners who had replied to their foes' attacks with their sixty-pounder guns. French artillerymen who had manned the ferocious 75 mm field guns which threw up to twenty rounds a minute at German trenches now shared glasses of wine with their former battlefield foes.

The fields of desolation were now endless acres of pristine vegetation. Row upon row of red and green grapes, luscious crisp apples, bright yellow sunflowers, rich burgundy roses and poppies forced one to utilize the depths of their visionary prowess in order to take in the whole panorama of divine agricultural bliss. For those who had orchestrated long hours of shrilling destruction and abnormal fear which drove men in the trenches mad, this was a moment they had dreamed about daily during the Great War of industrialized murder.

Such was the devastation wrought by the artillery throughout the conflict that the operators of the devil's mechanical reapers had asked for absolution from their crimes against humanity even after they had been absolved of any wrongdoing upon their entrance through the Gates of St. Peter. Nothing had been responsible for more battlefield deaths than the technological behemoths which contributed to the stalemate of the trenches forcing men to endure four years of slaughter. Many of those listed as "Unknown" or "Missing in

Action" had been buried or shredded by shells which moved tons of earth at a time or sliced the human body into pieces and slivers that even modern-day forensics couldn't identify.

The unspoken guilt still felt by the gunners was understood most by the one who sat in the middle of them as they quietly reflected on the beauty and serenity that was in front of them, conflicting with the thoughts of all the horror they had inflicted on their fellow humans. Jesus felt their anguish, as well as their deep regret. Embracing their God-given empathy was their strength which more than made up for their human weaknesses of blind obedience to political leaders and hateful nationalism. The quiet nature of their love for their fellow man was glorious.

10

In the Glory of God dining hall, one of the vast number of banquet halls which dotted the heavenly landscape, a young German soldier sat at the end of a long table, his head and back resting against the wall. He had eaten his fill of fresh fruits and being a light eater, washed it down with cool, sparkling Angel Water, the local brand personally endorsed by St. Peter as well as the apostles.

A young boy of eight years approached him with a plate of raspberry fudge cake, topped with a thick white icing decorated in the shape of swirls. A pitted cherry rested atop his delectable treasure.

"This is for you," he said unabashed. "I want to thank you."

Armin leaned forward, his curiosity piqued.

"I remember you taking a picture of me and my family as the government troops were marching us away from our home."

His mouth opened but evoked no sound. He sat stupefied as his mind raced back to that awful moment, but Armin knew what the happy child in front of him was talking about.

During the war, Armin Wegner had been in Turkey and had not only witnessed the persecution of the Armenians, which in retrospect was the first Holocaust of the twentieth century, but he had secretly filmed some of its worst acts of inhumanity. Though few in number, his covert photographs helped educate the world to one of the hidden atrocities in a war of continual highly publicized atrocities.

"I didn't realize anyone saw me taking those photographs," he began. "I was so scared I would get in trouble, but I felt so hollow not being able to stop what I was witnessing." Armin's eyes dropped down toward the floor, afraid of the response he would hear from his next inquiry. "What happened to you after you saw me taking a picture of you?"

Without hesitation, the boy replied, "We were marched to a camp beyond our town, and my parents were shot by the soldiers. I don't know why they let me live, but within a few weeks I starved to death. They never gave us anything to eat or drink."

Armin's eyes welled up. "I'm sorry I didn't do anything to help you that day," he said in an apologetic tone. "I'm sorry the world did nothing," he offered up in a more regretful tone.

"My name is Mehemet," said the boy in a very straightforward manner. He pushed his dessert closer toward Armin. "I love cake of any kind. Up here it seems I can eat as much as I want, so I want to share some with you." His spirit and smile was contagious.

"Are your parents here, Mehemet?" Armin asked as he took a forkful of the soft, spongy baked good. The icing melted against the roof of his mouth and the taste of an abundance of sugar made his eyes pop.

"Yes, they are at another table talking with other people from our town who were also killed by the Turkish soldiers. I told them about you, and they hope to meet you later. They said they didn't see you there the day you took pictures of us. I guess I was the only one."

Armin took a swig of Angel Water and pushed the remainder of the cake back toward Mehemet's side of the table. "That is too rich for me, my young friend. Thank you for your kindness."

"You are welcome. My parents taught me to reward kindness with kindness. When nobody else was helping us, you did the best you could to care about us."

Armin smiled at the wisdom of the youngster. For the first time since he witnessed the events of the Armenian Holocaust by the Turks he felt a sense of accomplishing something positive. In the midst of a great hatred, he had never realized he had been participating in teaching a child such a beautiful lesson. It made him feel satisfied that he had accomplished something positive in his life.

11

One of the most extraordinary reunions among the millions of reunions occurring throughout the vastness of God's Kingdom involved those who had never known one another, with few exceptions, in the land of the living. In the bureaucracy of all armies there resided one group after another whose responsibilities were important for the functioning of the armies as they prepared for combat and their eventual involvement in battle. But a small group, compared with the overall numbers which made up the militaries of all of the combatant nations, had a unique task.

The Graves Registration Units, as they were commonly called, carried out their labor in the quiet aftermath of the viciousness of any engagement. Theirs was a unique situation. First and foremost, the deceased had to be recovered from their place of earthly departure. Where a soldier died was as vast as the circumstances that contributed to his death.

Some died on the table during surgery, as doctors and nurses, with steadfast and methodical skills, did everything in their power to ward off the Reaper. But the reality of a wounded soldier was that many times more blood poured forth from their body than could be staunched or replaced, and they died surrounded by intelligent medical technicians with the best intentions of saving them.

Some died while lying in their hospital cots, recovering from their wounds despite the operations performed on them by heroic surgeons and nurses.

Some fell from the sky from thousands of feet high burning to death in their new flying contraptions that were rarely if ever outfitted with parachutes. Sometimes they fell out of their planes and their bodies thumped into the hard ground like rocks, leaving an imprint on Mother Earth while their shattered bodies littered the landscape.

Some died in No Man's Land while on night patrol after they slithered their way into a shell hole seeking protection from the night shelling or the machine gun fire of a scared sentry. What they believed was an uninhabited refuge turned out to be the place where they gasped their last breath as a startled enemy already occupying the hole was quicker to plunge a knife into their ribcage or belly and gut him. When he didn't return from patrol, he was listed as missing in action.

Some died under tons of soil which collapsed on top of them while they hid in a dugout enduring another artillery barrage. When they were dug out to be reburied, another absurdity of warfare, their mouth and nose were clogged with soil.

Some died in the trenches from a well-placed sniper bullet that tore through their forehead and blew out the back of their skull spewing brain matter in all directions.

Huge numbers died on the battlefield after they exposed themselves from the safety of their well-entrenched positions to participate in another frontal attack that throughout the entirety of the war they had been told by their commanders and leaders would be the attack to end the war.

Recovering the deceased was in the hands of the Graves Registration Units, or more plainly, the gravediggers.

Robert Middleton of the 1st Unit of the King's Guardian Corps and Douglass Tyson of the American 1st Division, 2nd Graves Registration Unit, spotted one another while they were reviewing the throngs of people passing them by as they sat in front of the Chapel of the Holy Mother. While sitting at angled benches opposite one another, they made eye contact numerous times as their necks twisted left and right trying to identify any of those walking by as someone they once laid to rest. Douglass finally made his way over to Robert and sat beside him on the pearly white wooden bench seated in the shade of a lovely yellow-green leafed elm tree.

"I assume we are in the same boat, eh, mate?" he joked. "I can't recognize anyone, and from the look on your face, neither can you."

"I'm Robert Middleton of the King's burial corps. When we were burying them they were nameless bodies, up here, I can really see the individuality of each person."

"I'm Douggie Tyson, Yankee Graves Registration. I tried to treat them as individuals while we were burying them, but there were so many of them . . ." His sentence trailed off in the light breeze which tapped their cheeks as they sat there and began to reminisce.

"It's not that we ever disrespected any of the boys, it was that it just became so mechanical after awhile, almost like working on an assembly line, like your Henry Ford making all those Model Ts."

"After one hour on the job I threw up worse than I ever did in my life," Douglass said in a matter-of-fact manner. "I tried to wash the blood off of a young private's face. I just kept thinking that his mother somewhere back in the states would appreciate that, though she would never know anyway. It just seemed like the right thing to do, to bury him with some dignity. Anyway, I poured a little water on his face and began to wipe away the blood with a cloth, and I began to realize as the blood wouldn't wipe away that I wasn't wiping his skin anymore. The shrapnel had torn open the side of his face down to the bone. I could see his skull, well, his orbital bones. One of his eyes was missing, there was just a hole. I don't know why I didn't notice that when I first looked at him, I just never thought about someone getting his eye shot out."

Robert patted Douglass on the shoulder in order to comfort him and let him know he understood. It was something someone in their profession shared with one another every time they performed their duty.

"The ones who really bothered me were the lads I couldn't identify. My God there were so many of them after the first day of the Somme, and then attack after attack at Ypres and Loos. It was incomprehensible that so many of them, so many of them, so many of them . . . I know they had names, I know they were someone." He took a deep breath to settle himself and refocus.

"In the beginning, when I first started," said Douglass as he began another recollection, "I thought it would be a nice gesture to write down the name and address of the ones that could be identified," he sighed in dejection, "and then in my off hours I planned to write a letter of sympathy to their next of kin. I thought it might be nicer for someone back in the states to get a handwritten letter to go along with the typed form letter that the government would send out."

Robert offered up a gentle smile of approval. "That's a very significant act of kindness, Douggie. I'm sure it was most appreciated by those on the home front."

Douglass smirked. "I said I planned to do it, but I never sent one. I never thought about how overwhelming something like that would be. Maybe I could have sent a few during my off hours but I never got hours off, well, not like I thought I might get. My first day I spent more than eighteen hours processing bodies, cleaning them, writing down personal information, listing personal possessions of the deceased. You know the process, I imagine it wasn't that much different for you Brits."

"No, not that much different, mate," Robert replied somberly.

"When I went back to my quarters after that first shift, I was empty. I couldn't think of what to say to anyone, especially parents of dead soldiers, and I had never been so physically exhausted in my life, not to mention the mental exhaustion. All I know is that I slept until someone woke me the next day and then it started all over again. I think I spent all of my waking hours in Europe taking care of dead bodies . . . so many dead boys."

Robert handed Douglass a pristine white silk kerchief to damp away the emotions that had escaped his eyes. He patted his back once again in shared empathy.

"Excuse me, gentlemen," a meek voice interrupted their moment of solace.

They raised their heads simultaneously and found themselves staring at a young sandy-haired lad who didn't look any older than a sixteen-year-old schoolboy. He acknowledged Robert with a respectful nod and then reached out to procure a sturdy handshake from Douglass. Their eyes locked onto one another.

"I know you don't recognize me, sir," he began with an air of confidence and respect in his voice, "but I will never forget you or what you did for me. My face was a mess when they brought me to you, and I could only see you with the one eye that wasn't destroyed. I mean it's hard to explain, I was dead, but I could still see everything you did for me."

Douglass remained silent but his expression spoke volumes. It was tender.

"You were gentle with me, even after you got sick. I know I looked hideous, less than human with my face being nothing but blood and shredded skin, tissues and bone splinters. I could feel the compassion you had for my body, and I remember hearing you tell someone else that you wanted me presentable so my mother would be comforted. You preserved my dignity when the war did its best to deny me that even in death."

Douglass stood up and embraced the young soldier. Then he stepped back and looked him over. His blonde hair was short but wavy. He had a distinguished jaw that jutted out in a show of strength and character. His nose was short but pointed and his eyes . . . his eyes . . . both of them were so spectacularly sharp blue.

"It is so rewarding to see you here," said Douglass with a small quiver in his voice. "It is a joy to see you alive, and in the prime of your youth again."

"There are many of us, Douglass, and Robert," he said as he looked in his direction as well. "We have been wondering around different parts of heaven looking for all of you who took care of us in our moment of death. A large number of us were unidentified at the time of our demise and remained that way until now. I imagine that the two of you will be quite busy talking to all us over the next few months as we finally make your acquaintance under better and more joyous circumstances."

The young soldier's prediction didn't take long to materialize as a large throng of young men surrounded Douglass and Robert and began sharing with them their stories of death, and more importantly how they were treated with love at the time of their departing from their mortal life.

12

Making his way from "The Meadow of Peace and Meditation" after a long period of providing insight for many of the newly arrived, Jesus stopped at one of the water wells that dotted the endless paths of heaven to treat himself to some refreshment. As he retrieved a bucket from the depths of the well, he was met by a trio who seemed hesitant to vocalize their thoughts. Recognizing their lack of discourse, he offered them a drink.

"Please, it's Holy Trinity Water. It's said to be the best in heaven."

The tallest of the three grasped the ladle and took a healthy gulp. As it hit the back of his throat the chilling sensation sent a jolt of satisfaction throughout his taste buds. He finished the contents of the dipper and handed it to the man next to him but not before commenting, "Oh my, they should call that miracle water. I've never had something so invigorating and enjoyably tasty."

The remaining duo enjoyed the same experience as Jesus was able to chip in his endorsement while they slaked their thirst. "I think it's the best in heaven, though I hear St. Peter and the apostles keep telling others that Angel Water is the supreme drink in our eternal world."

They all shared a round of laughter and being a little less apprehensive than they were moments earlier, they began their query of God's son.

"Teacher, my name is Nikolai Yevgeny. My friends are Reinhard Kleist and Nigel Chapman. We hesitate to ask but we are trying to understand why we are here."

Jesus allowed himself to slump down against the wall of the water well, his legs outstretched as he made himself comfortable. The knowledge-seeking trio sat cross-legged in an arc in front of him.

Jesus was very straightforward with them. "What did each of you do in the war?"

"We were all snipers," answered Nikolai as Reinhard and Nigel nodded in agreement.

"You were soldiers, as were so many of your generation. This is your eternal reward for your suffering on earth." Jesus knew his answer would not be sufficient for them as he studied their faces while they analyzed his response.

"But we killed so many," Nigel evoked as the other two bowed their heads in shame. "We waited, sometimes hours, hidden among the debris of the trenches or the camouflage of the countryside in order to get one perfect shot at an unsuspecting or careless soldier."

"Their deaths were not pleasant either," Reinhard weighed in. "They were head shots, all of them. We would splatter someone's head like a ripe piece of fruit, and then we would slither away from our concealed positions like snakes."

"I killed over a hundred men," Nikolai confessed. "I quit counting after I killed my hundredth, because I didn't want to know anymore how many lives I ended."

Jesus studied them.

"Did you kill with malice?" he asked dryly.

There was a prolonged silence.

Jesus made figures in the dirt with a stick while they evaluated their behaviors during the war.

"No, I did not," stated Nikolai. "I can unequivocally say no. Yes, I did see the Germans as my enemies who were invading Mother Russia. I wanted to kill as many as I could in order to protect my country. I only killed soldiers who were armed and were in a position to defend themselves or kill my comrades."

"I killed because I was trained to kill enemies of the Kaiser," admitted Reinhard in a sullen tone. "I can say with truthfulness that I did not kill for the enjoyment or the pleasure of killing. Even when I was given a medal for my actions, I did not find pleasure in what

I had done. In fact, after I was awarded my Iron Cross, I started to question why I was considered a hero. I didn't consider hiding in foliage or under a piece of discarded sheet metal waiting to shoot an unaware enemy soldier who wasn't shooting back at me an act of heroism."

Jesus scribbled a few more circles and triangles on the ground which raised a little dust. He gazed at Nigel.

"I did," he said slowly. "I killed with malice." Nikolai and Reinhard showed no emotion in response to Nigel's declaration. Neither of them looked in his direction as they maintained their focus on Jesus.

"My brother was killed early in the war by the Germans. I wanted to kill all of them to avenge my brother. I hated them."

"Your truthfulness is respected," stated Jesus. "The feelings of the heart are true. Your love for your brother was a great blessing for your mother and father."

"But I know my feelings were evil. I hated. I had the ability to love and I chose to hate."

"What happened to you after the war?" Jesus inquired.

Nigel's head drooped. "I lived in anger and regret. My brother was dead and nothing I could do would bring him back. I began to realize nothing changed that fact simply because I killed so many German soldiers. I found myself many times wondering how many brothers of brothers I had killed, or how many young children I left fatherless because of my hatred and desire to kill and inflict pain on others." He stopped and they sat in silence.

Then Nigel continued.

"I began to cry in public when I would see children with their parents or siblings. I knew somewhere in Germany there were dozens and dozens and dozens of children who were not experiencing that joy and wonder of life because of me. I couldn't face that anymore. I shut myself in from the world. I never left my home so I wouldn't have to see children anywhere. I never married nor had children of my own."

Nikolai and Reinhard patted Nigel on his shoulder or rubbed his head in gestures of mutual assurance.

Jesus looked their way.

"What happened to each of you after the war?"

Nikolai delayed a second before responding. "I was killed before the end of the war. I set off a booby trap one day and my arm was blown off. I bled to death before anyone could help me. I was alone. I died alone.

"I was killed also," said Reinhard. "A few days before the armistice was declared, so close to going home. I was careless. I raised my head and an enemy sniper, some Tommy or Scot like Nigel here, shot me clean through the forehead. I never saw my wife and two boys again."

Jesus rose and drew himself another ladle of Holy Trinity Water. The trio rose as well and stood before him.

"Each of you has already suffered for your actions. The spirit of reconciliation has shown itself within you. My Father's Kingdom is not about punishment and suffering but about eternal salvation. Welcome to His house. Seek out your families and loved ones, they are waiting for you."

13

The strangeness of feeling whole again had not yet passed. Edward Thomas ran his hands up and down his legs and his chest for what seemed like the hundredth time. He wiggled his fingers then softly brushed them across his fresh skinned cheeks. He slowly peeked into the circular hand mirror he had carried with him in the trenches. Sheepishly he smiled back at himself in the reflection.

Early in 1917 he had disintegrated amidst an intense artillery barrage. The official telegram from the British Imperial War Office to his new wife back in London had in cold, bureaucratic terms informed her that he had been killed in action on the western front while in military action in defense of the King's Empire. While its tone was void of emotion and specifics, it saved his beautiful bride of eight weeks the ugliness that might otherwise have occupied her thoughts the next sixty some years of her life which she spent alone without him.

As they say, there wasn't enough of him left to bury. Some of his pals had seen him shortly before the hundreds of pounds of explosives and steel had spread his arms and legs about the battle-field. But the problem they encountered afterward was they couldn't positively identify any of the extremities they found as belonging to her betrothed. The shell that decimated Edward did the same to another sixteen privates and a corporal. Survivors had found twenty-nine arms, twenty-eight legs, and thirteen heads all separate from their bodies. The damage to their faces was so severe that only one of them could be positively identified by comrades who sifted through the human debris field. Most heads had eyes missing or hair scorched off and skin that had shriveled like plastic placed before the flame of a blowtorch. Gathered arms were missing fingers and legs were absent not only of uniforms and boots but toes. For sanitary reasons the soldiers at the front buried the remnants of their brothers-in-arms in a mass grave, offered their final thoughts and prayers to them, and continued on with themselves trying to stay alive for another day.

When Helen read the news of Edward's death she collapsed in front of the post carrier who had delivered the evil note. When she awoke a day later in the hospital she was informed that the child she was carrying was also lost. She mourned her beloved husband and honored his memory and their love the rest of her life by never remarrying, let alone dating another. She sought solace in her faith, praying to God each day that Edward's soul would be accepted into heaven and that when they met again they would be able to continue sharing their love forever.

Now, that time had come. It was another element of The Grand Reunion that was happening a thousandfold throughout the celestial kingdom and in the countless ways that love is expressed and enables it for all time to conquer the deception of darkness and evil.

Heaven presented the young couple with a story book setting as was fitting the sweetness of their love. Edward lightly tapped on the door of the cottage with his left hand. The gentle sensation of feeling his knuckles encounter the soft wood of the door brought a feeling of satisfaction that tingled throughout his mind and body. To be a whole human again, with the sense of touch, it was . . .

His thoughts were stifled as the door opened and Helen greeted him with her ebullient smile that had allowed him to drift off to sleep in the mental warmth of her love so many cold nights while serving at the front. Her long, brown hair curled around her shoulders and the soft, yellow, flowered dress that adorned her feminine features sent emotions of sentiment coursing through his vibrant, virile, youthful body.

Their love which had never ended, which death could not destroy, was rekindled with the passion that had initially led them to marry one another. The true joy of their life together would be their heavenly blessing. Within the next few years they would christen the fruits of their marriage Faith, Joseph, Claire, Michael, and Anna Marie.

14

The snow fell quietly. It came down soft and gentle. It actually fluttered as the prose presented it in so many children's tales.

There was no sound of accompanying wind to distract the witnesses from the intense beauty of the endless steppes which showcased another vision of God's majestic touch of artistry.

"Who knew that white could come in so many colors?" a soft-spoken Ivan Kharkov softly asked to no one in particular, though the thought may very well have been shared by the endless multitudes who had gathered in this part of heaven to enjoy what had been taken from them by the war.

The large snowflakes that graciously descended were a virgin white that sparkled as they twisted on their downward course to reunite with the millions which had preceded them. As they reached their mates, they gently laid upon them as if providing comfort. A glint of sun would create a vibrant white that sparkled like a pristine diamond on the hand of a newly engaged fiancé.

The canvas of the sensually soothing scene was unblemished. Under the bright fallen crystalline glitter lay land no longer desiccated by war. Gone were the pockmarked shell holes which had shredded the continuity of nature. Rolling fields of tall, yellow-green blades of grass still poked through the accumulated snowfall, though in time that would be a battle that would be peacefully lost to the descending snow.

Ivan closed his eyes and inhaled deeply. He savored the feeling. The freshness of the cold warmed his heart. Gone from his memory were the pangs of the biting cold which had slowly killed him years before on the Eastern Front. The winter of 1917–1918 had ushered in the cadavers of hundreds of thousands of forlorn men who had been abandoned by their Czar. Along with many fighting a war without weapons, their government had betrayed their loyalty without supplying them sufficient amounts of food or proper winter clothing. Feeling his stomach rumble from pangs of hunger and his body quiver from the intensity of the cold, Ivan had experienced the frostbite which denied him his feet and when too weak to march any further, or offer up any more verbal curses to His Majesty, he had laid down, his body shivering up to the last minutes before he froze to death.

When Ivan opened his eyes he could see flakes dancing on the tip of his nose before silently moisturizing from his body heat. To his right children by the score frolicked about the majestic playground. He couldn't identify any of them but in his heart knew that they were most likely some of the children who had died that same winter that he passed. War usually killed more children than adults. They seemed to freeze to death or starve to death a lot faster than your average adult. A quick smile rolled over his face as he found pleasure in watching them enjoy their childhoods once again.

"This is such a special place," said a stranger who had approached Ivan without him noticing until the man sat down beside him.

"Very much so," responded Ivan without breaking eye contact from the children he was observing.

"Do you remember when we used to play like that?" inquired his company.

For the first time since sitting in the cold, Ivan felt a chill permeate his body. It was his little brother's voice from so long ago. He turned sideways, already in the process of bringing his arms around to give him a hug that had been repeated by millions of others that day. Instead of rising to embrace one another, they ended up rolling forward down the small incline in front of them. They were covered with enough snow that they looked like giant polar bears when they stood erect.

"I have missed you very much, Andrei," Ivan finally blurted out.

"I knew I would find you here today," Andrei said in a casual tone. "It is so nice to enjoy the kindness of nature instead of its harsh, unbridled anger."

"I am sorry I never got back home from the war," Ivan apologized.

"Mother and Father figured that you died when you didn't come back after the surrender at Brest-Litovsk to the Germans. I didn't last too much longer myself. Food was scarce, and the cold just kept biting away at my strength, not much a fourteen-year-old could do against two great opponents." He paused to remember sadly. "Starving to death is the end result of most warfare, so much pity to bestow upon children."

"But we are here now," said Ivan heartily. "Let us find Mother and Father and we can celebrate."

"Agreed," Andrei concurred as he looked out over the fields in front of them, "but I want to enjoy this a little while longer." He took a deep breath and sighed with contentment. "How beautiful. Who knew white could come in so many colors?"

Ivan smiled with great satisfaction as they both sat down in the snow again to enjoy the silent rapture of nature's talent. The dazzling bright white that rested on the tips of branches flickered like Christmas lights bedecked for the celebration of the baby Jesus. Looking up against the backdrop of the gray winter sky, the descending flakes morphed from hard to see droplets into infinite shapes of glazed frozen crystals. The mosaic of shades combined to create a portrait of romanticized winter perfection. The smiles on the faces of Ivan and his younger brother reflected their feelings of joyous simplicity.

15

It is hard for the reader who has not experienced the want of food to the point that obtaining it would challenge your values to understand the internal combat one goes through as a result of trying to survive on a battlefield. Living in the trenches kept one's nerves on end, never knowing when a single shell may mark the prelude to thousands of accompanying high explosive missiles for hours on end. One walked or crept with a hunch in his posture always cognizant that even exposing a few inches of one's head may offer a sniper the perfect target he had been waiting for in patient anticipation for hours on end. The morning mist may be confused with a gas attack having been launched and panic would momentarily ensue as one desperately tried to fit his gas mask in place. A few hours of rain would fill the bottoms of trenches with inches and sometimes feet of water that one had to tread until the engineers would pump it out. Even then more often than not there was a puddle of water every few feet which helped contribute to unsanitary living conditions for the men, though it was joy for the insects to breed in prior to them hitching rides on the backs of the endless population of rats that seemed to bivouac in the trenches. The armies of vermin outnumbered the soldiers of every belligerent nation involved in the war.

Combat consumed the strength of individuals at a voracious rate. The adrenaline drained their bodies of nutrients in the highly charged moments of attempting to kill the enemy while simultaneously trying to save one's own life. Such was the situation Noah Johnson found himself in after the rest of his patrol had either been killed or had retreated from the scene of yet another useless skirmish between Australian and German troops in some obscure nameless wooded area along the battlefront.

Noah took a slow, deep breath in order to calm himself. He was alive, which was comforting. His eyes surveyed the surrounding geography. He was alone, which was discomforting. He was alone in the sense that he was the only living body within his field of vision. Within the vicinity of the fallen tree he was lying against for protection were the dead bodies of three comrades and one young lad who died for his Kaiser. The German soldier was so close Noah could reach out and touch him. He didn't recall seeing the enemy soldier during the fighting.

The corpses of the Australians were all face down. Noah could see the exit holes of the bullets which had taken their lives. One had six, another seven, and the third fifteen. Their torsos looked like sieves. He closed his eyes momentarily to reflect on the odds of himself having not been hit once though the men he had just looked upon were all behind him during their advance.

Upon opening his eyes he noticed the dead German soldier was lying on his back looking skyward. Half of his face had been sheared away. He was grotesque in his death. Noah studied the rest of the lad's body. His kit bag still attached to his waist and held in place by a shoulder strap seemed to bulge with a fair amount of food, though for the moment Noah couldn't tell what delightful morsels they might be. He realized at that moment how much his body yearned for nourishment.

Noah reached for his own mess kit but quickly realized it was no longer attached to his uniform. Doing a once over of his own self the only piece of equipment still in place on his person was an ammunition belt filled with a half dozen or so unused clips of rifle ammunition. He swore quietly under his breath.

He felt a hollow pang in his stomach. His eyes gravitated back to the dead German. His conscience was already telling him it wasn't right to take food from the dead. He didn't want to desecrate the deceased any more than the war had already done. Hours lingered by until daylight had retired.

Maybe there is fresh bread or a piece of fruit in his kit, Noah found himself thinking over and over again.

The inner struggle continued through the night and into the early morning hours of the next day. As the sun was peeking over the horizon with darkness still clinging to its majority possession of the sky, Noah realized he had spent the entire night awake, silently arguing with himself whether to take the food from the dead soldier. As the sun gained more altitude, Noah thought about his last meal more than twenty-four hours earlier.

His stomach reminded the remainder of his body that it was in want of a new meal. Slowly Noah leaned his body away from the fallen tree which he had been propped against all these hours and gently let his body slump to the ground. Now on his side he inched his way the couple feet over to the deceased German.

"God forgive me," he recited quietly three times, the last time the words escaping his lips his hands were already tugging loose from the day-old corpse his whole food kit. With the stealth that would rival a barn owl swooping down on his unsuspecting prey, Noah retrieved the gray sack and quickly repositioned his body within the safety of the fallen tree.

Almost salivating in anticipation he pushed the sides of the kit in opposite directions and slowly reached in to retrieve its contents. The bread was shaped like a block but it hadn't been cut or even gnawed on. It had a hard outside shell but when Noah ripped off a hunk it exposed a soft interior. He slipped a piece into his mouth and relished the taste of sustenance for the first time in over a day. He couldn't exactly place the flavor but it reminded him of a rye bread he used to periodically purchase from a local market back home before the war.

Noah's next find, wrapped in some coarse paper, was a sausage link. Like the status of the bread, it was pristine. Noah thought for a second that the poor soul he took the food from didn't even have time for a last meal on his last day on earth. That thought was fleeting, however, as Noah dumped the remaining contents of the kit in his lap. A small square piece of some type of cheese, two apples, a small potato, and of all things an orange lay cradled within the confines of his outstretched legs.

The orange was bigger than the two apples combined. Noah cupped it in his hands and slowly rubbed it against the side of his face. It was soft and exotic. He hadn't seen an orange in over six months, not since he had shipped out from the land down under. His index finger broke through the skin and allowed him to peel back a large part of the rind. He enjoyed the time it took to uncover the whole of the interior of the fruit. When it was ready to eat, he pulled it apart one slice at a time and consumed it the same way. He laid each piece on his tongue and then crushed it against the roof of his mouth, letting the newly released juice squirt to all parts of his mouth. His taste buds were working in overdrive. They hadn't enjoyed anything so sweet and sugary in months. When he got to the last piece he closed his eyes before slipping it into his mouth and savored the moment by just letting it sit on his tongue a little while longer before finally consuming it.

After the last swallow of orange he turned his attention to the apples. One of the two had inadvertently rolled down his legs while he had been lost in the passion of enjoying the vitamin rejuvenating fruit and was resting no more than a foot away from the heel of his boot. As he reached forward to retrieve it he exposed just enough of his head from the security of the fallen tree and the unseen sniper who had been patiently watching him throughout the morning hours delivered a shot that blew out the right side of his cranium.

After the initial euphoria of entering into heaven had receded, but only by a bit, they found themselves as if some unseen force had drawn them there, in Saint Dorothy Orchards, located in close proximity to the Garden of Eden. It was truly a unique place. The Saint Dorothy Orchards were interspersed with every kind of orange and apple ever known. No other fruit was grown here. The angels joked that when the garden was designed Jesus specifically required that contrary to what others had argued about for years be settled forever by mixing apples and oranges. It was believed that when Jesus was a little boy in the temple teaching about his Father in heaven, the Pharisees had tried to trip him up by asking whether or not God's message to love one another was possible since some people were evil and imbued with the message of Satan. Jesus had responded to them by saying that we are all God's children even though all people were sinners. One of the Pharisees was flippant in his response that believers in God's word and sinners could never be one and the same in that it was like mixing apples and oranges. The angels always chuckled among themselves that the Saint Dorothy Orchards was Jesus's way of getting in the last word, and the last laugh. It was reflective of the acerbic sense of humor which Jesus possessed.

Noah's senses were in aromatic overdrive as he walked among the endless interspersed rows of Galas, Clementines, Red and Golden Delicious, tangerines, Fuji, honey tangerines, Granny Smiths, cara carras, Honeycrisp, tangelos, Braeburn, navels, Ambrosia, blood oranges, Autumn Glory, Satsumas, Aurora . . . it was a honeybees' never-ending fantasy.

By the time Noah traversed the first acre of fruity delights, he met and was reunited with those individuals who were part of his last day alive. The three Australian countrymen who had met their demise before he even realized they had been killed, the German soldier who he liberated his last edible bites from, including the succulent orange, and the sniper who had made him pay with his life for want of reaching for an errant apple which had rolled beyond his grasp. They shared handshakes and smiles and laughter, sat down among their Eden of fruit, and reminisced.

"I hoped you would make it, mate," said Cooper, one of the three Aussies, the one who had been shot more than a dozen times.

Oliver and Jack, the other two killed in the same episode, nodded in agreement.

Albrecht, the German soldier who Noah took the food kit from, tossed Noah a fresh tangelo he had just picked from the branch hanging over his head.

"I'm sorry I killed you," Jurgen, the former sniper, apologized. "I was so hungry. I hadn't eaten for two days. I caught glimpses of you enjoying that orange but never enough to get a finishing shot at you until you exposed yourself reaching for that apple. I want you to know that I didn't take your life out of hatred. I did it out of despair.

I crawled my way over to you after I finished you off to retrieve that apple. When I signed up to fight, I never realized I would be more inclined to kill another man in order to get a bit of food from him rather than for his nationalistic beliefs."

"It's not your fault," quipped Jack with his thick accent.

"I don't blame you for killing me," said Noah, looking toward Jurgen. "It was my own dumb, careless fault."

"It's none of our faults," followed Oliver with his commentary. "We were gullible enough to fight for the slogans and thoughts of glory which misled us in our youthful indiscretions."

As they ate from the apple and orange trees which embraced the locale of their get together they shared moments of satisfaction and contentment being in each other's company. It was peaceful and they reveled in the humanity which the war had taken from them in the days of their youth.

"Whose fault do you think it was?" asked Jurgen in a serious tone that momentarily distracted their moments of glee.

"That's for God to decide," Noah answered. "I'm sure those accountable for what they did to us will get their just comeuppance. I won't find any joy in it, but I'm sure that what God will decide for them will be just."

Without any forward notice a large Honeycrisp fell onto Noah's head, bringing a round of laughter from the gathering of young lads. It distracted them from the serious tone their conversation had been heading in and the diversion opened up a wave of jokes amongst them about everything from how hard Noah's head must be to maybe it was a sign from God to change the topic of discussion to something more lighthearted and pleasurable.

Maybe the latter view was true. God wanted them to focus on the joy of being together in His house. The wrath of His power upon those who would be held accountable for the war would be something no one would want to witness.

16

October 21, 1918
Brookville, Pennsylvania

My Dear Jimmy,

I haven't heard anything from you in over a
month but I am only thinking the best like you told
me to do in your previous letters. The newspapers
are saying there has been a lot of heavy fighting and
the Germans are on the run, which I hope means
that you will be coming home soon. I hope when this
is over we will never be separated again. Your little angel Nicole gives your picture a kiss every night
before I put her down to sleep. I keep telling her we
will be seeing you soon but I don't think a five-year-
old really understands. I can barely understand why
we have to be apart, I hope all the problems that
led to our country becoming involved in this war
will be settled once it is over. I hope you are getting
enough to eat and that you are able to stay warm
and not catch cold. We had some snow flurries the
other night and I can feel winter starting to creep in.

I miss you to the point that it hurts and though
I don't want to upset you, I cry many nights sitting
alone after tucking in Nicole. I told you I would

be strong for you while you were away, and I am keeping my promise. I don't think crying is a sign of weakness. I think it's another way of saying how much I love you. I will keep praying for you.

I love you always
Trisha

When she finished reading the old, dog-eared letter, she smiled at her beloved as she folded it back up and placed it in the yellowing envelope. Nicole had both her arms securely wrapped around her dad's neck as he held her cupped against his body with his right forearm. He kissed their precious daughter on the top of the head but she remained sleeping. Trisha tucked the envelope back in her purse and retrieved another one that didn't look any different from the one she just deposited in her shoulder bag. She reached up for Nicole with the envelope protruding from her hand.

"Your turn, Jimmy," she said in the most pleasant of voices.

They transferred Nicole effortlessly as they had done numerous times since the early part of the day when they first began reading their wartime letters to one another. It was a promise they had made with one another the day before Jimmy had left for basic training at Fort Dix. They had joked so many times about how funny and corny the letters would sound to them in the years after the war when they were enjoying their older years of life together. They had written almost a hundred letters between them, from the time Jimmy left for boot camp until he returned early in 1919 after finishing up occupation duty in France and Germany. They had been married six years at the time Jimmy was drafted into the army.

Jimmy smiled at the letter he picked to read.

"I remember writing this one. It was the night before one of our attacks against the German lines. Let me see." He began reading to Trisha.

October 30, 1918.

My lovely Trisha,

Thank you for your last correspondence. Your words and thoughts bring more comfort to me than you realize. I told you I would never lie to you and the truth is I am rather frightened at the thought of going into combat. Since I've been here we have exchanged a lot of artillery fire with the Huns but we haven't gone over the top yet to rush their lines and kill them face to face. I don't know what that will be like and I hope that when it happens it won't contribute to making me a hard man. I know my job is to kill enemy soldiers, but after being in the trenches for even a couple of weeks, I assume that the German soldier is experiencing the same lifestyle that I am, but on the other hand if it weren't for them I wouldn't be here in Europe so far away from you and our lovely Nicole.

My heart yearns for your company. It is getting colder and colder each night and it reminds me of how much I miss being warmed by you in front of the fireplace. When I daydream to reduce the boredom of trench life, I find great comfort in remembering the pleasure of a gentle kiss you might offer me when waking me in the morning or saying goodbye as I left our house for work that day. I know the more I write the more homesick I make myself. Please pray that this war will soon be over and we may resume our life together once again.

I love you always and I will always be your darling Jimmy.

They exchanged loving smiles with one another as Jimmy replaced the letter in its century-old envelope. He retrieved another one to read so Trisha could momentarily limit the routine of handing Nicole back and forth. Jimmy flicked open another of their romantic literary treasures.

November 3, 1918

My beautiful and adorable Trisha,

I find solace in sitting here and scribbling these lines to you. I ask your forgiveness and understanding if you find my handwriting difficult to interpret. I can feel nerves jumping as I write but my mind is so full of thoughts that I want to impart them to you before I forget everything I would like to say to you.

I never know how much time I will have to write between all the events which seem to be happening without letup. I am so happy to be alive after what we went through in the last thirty-six hours, though I am not sure that I will ever truly be able to explain to you or anyone for that matter what exactly took place. I would rather experience my worst nightmares in the midst of an evening sleep than remember or recall things my eyes witnessed and my senses were forced to behold. I never knew that death could be visited upon humans in so many vile and wicked ways. It causes the strongest among us to tremble long after the fighting has concluded. It is violence beyond comprehension even for those of us who are perpetrating it.

As I take a breath to calm myself, I am able to expunge the scenes of combat from my mind and replace them with you. When I see you smile I am happy. I see my favorite image of a gentle breeze off the riverbank where we picnicked so many times quietly toss your light brown hair from one side to

*the other. I am in a state of solace once again. I am
so happy to be alive, to tell you over and over again
how much I love you and how much to be able to
just sit here and write these words makes me love
you so much more than I could possibly ever have
imagined. There are so many who I knew just yesterday and even this morning that no longer have
that luxury. I hope their loved ones will be able to
grasp life without them.*

*We are getting orders to move out again, as it
looks like another attack is imminent. I wish you
were in my arms so I could feel the warmth of your
love. I love you always and will always be your darling Jimmy.*

"I remember getting that one around Christmas," Trisha quietly
stated, not wanting to disturb the slumber of their angel. "I remember reading it and crying. I knew you were safe because the war was
over by that point but those things you said about what you saw on
the battlefield left me with a feeling that even though you were alive,
I might not be getting the same Jimmy back who went off to fight
and I was afraid I wouldn't know how to help you readjust."

"I was afraid of that myself," Jimmy said with a flicker of a
smile. "Who knew what happened would happen, right?"

Trisha was able to maneuver her free hand while still holding
on to Nicole in order to retrieve another letter. Her hand trembled a
little while she read it aloud as the two of them relived another horror
of the war that was visited on them as well as millions of others.

March 10, 1919

My dear Jimmy,

*I can hardly stop my hand from quivering as
I write. It has been a week now since I wrote last
about the fever that has intruded into our lives.*

Our angel Nicole shakes and burns from this incipient influenza. So many have died already across the country and Europe as indicated in the news reports and I can't help but wonder if a terrible fate awaits us as well. I highly doubt that this would be happening if it had not been for this war which has consumed so much of humanity these last four years. Never again will things be the same no matter how much we wish them to be. The doctor does not have good news to share with us. I pray that you will be here soon in order to hold our beloved daughter close to your heart and know her beautiful grace and smile one last time.

I have no other way of telling you these things without damaging your emotions. The effects of the war continue to keep us apart geographically but not in heart. You have been a flawless husband and father. Our time together I have treasured since first laying eyes upon you at the church dance those many summers ago. From the time we first held hands I knew what it meant to be in love, and it is an emotion that has never subsided in me despite the time of separation the war has forced upon us. I know we will meet again on the other side and our love will be as fresh and strong as it is at the moment I write these last words to you.

Thank you for loving me and making my life more beautiful that I can ever have imagined it would be.

I will always be your loving Trisha just as you will always remain my darling Jimmy.

Jimmy wiped away a few tears as he recalled those dark days.

"I was preparing to board ship and come back to you and Nicole when I got called into the captain's office and he told me that the two of you had succumbed to the influenza. I was holding it together pretty good until he informed me that for health reasons you and Nicole would be buried well before I arrived back in the United States."

Nicole began to stir and her eyes opened. Trisha put her down and she went over and grabbed Jimmy's hand. With the simplistic innocence of a five-year-old she informed her teary-eyed father, "There's no reason for you and Mommy to cry, Daddy. We're in heaven now and we will always be together."

A couple of the angels who had been watching Jimmy and Trisha read their letters and relive the events of the war brushed tears from their watering eyes. Sometimes it took the words of the children to help the adults make sense out of everything they were experiencing. Heaven was only a place for tears of joy and while the memories of those burdensome and painful days remained prevalent especially with newcomers, in time the depravities of the past would be replaced by all that was wholesome and good in the House of the Lord.

The war had unfairly punished them, inflicting pain and death upon the human forms of Trisha and Nicole along with bringing decades of lonesomeness and anguish to the remaining years of Jimmy's life. However, their faith, love, and commitment which they had pledged to one another on the day they exchanged their vows had led them home to their eternal reward.

17

The words of the poem were eloquent and beautiful, and they reflected the compassion and emotions the author had for the men he had served with and seen die before he joined them in death himself.

"Rouge Bouquet"
by Joyce Kilmer

In a wood they call Rouge Bouquet
There is a new-made grave today,
Built by never a spade nor pick
Yet covered with earth 10 meters thick.
There lie many fighting men,
Dead in their youthful prime,
Never to laugh nor love again
Nor taste the summertime.
For death came flying through the air
And stopped his flight at the dugout stair;
Touched his prey and left them there,
Clay to clay
He hid their bodies stealthily
In the soil of the land they fought to free
And fled away
Now over the grave abrupt and clear.
Three volleys ring;
And perhaps their brave young spirits hear

The bugles sing:
"Go to sleep!
Go to sleep"
Slumber well where the shell screamed and fell,
Let your rifles rest on the muddy floor,
You will not need them anymore.
Danger's past;
Now at last,
Go to sleep!"
There is on earth no worthier grave
To hold the bodies of the brave
Than this place of pain and pride
Where they nobly fought and nobly died.
Never fear but in the skies
Saints and angels stand
Smiling with their holy eyes
On the new-come band.
St. Michael's sword darts through the air
And touches the aureole on his hair
As he sees them standing saluting there,
His stalwart sons;
And Patrick, Brigid, Columkill
Rejoice that in veins of warriors still
The Gael's blood runs.
And up to Heaven's doorway floats,
From the wood called Rouge Bouquet,
A delicate cloud of bugle notes
That softly says:
"Farewell!
Farewell!"
Comrades true born anew, peace to you!
Your souls shall be where the heroes are
And your memory shines like the morning-star,
Brave and dear,
Shield us here.
Farewell!

The men in question belonged to the "Fighting 69th" regiment which was part of the American Rainbow Division. Early in 1918 they were in the trenches in the Rouge Bouquet sector and came under an intense German artillery barrage. The comrades Kilmer honored with his poem numbered twenty. The shell which found them had buried them under tons of mud, soil, and the wooden beams which had been part of their dugout. In desperation the survivors spent hours digging through the earth under which their friends had been so quickly buried. They were successful in retrieving only a quarter of the missing, being able to provide at least some of them with a decent burial. Mudslides due to the conditions of the trench and incessant bombing by the German artillery made continued attempts to recover their friends futile, and with heavy hearts the decision was made to cease further attempts.

At the memorial service held when the war took a respite, the regiment's beloved chaplain, Father Francis P. Duffy, read the poem Joyce Kilmer had written. The men openly wept for their brothers who had been taken from them in such an instant, in such quantity. In their idealism they had come to France to make the world safe for democracy and play their part in the war to end all wars. They had not come to conquer people or land, but to end oppression and restore peace. When they died it was not seen as in vain for their beliefs were just, but the sting of death knew nothing of ideals and honor as it brought only pain.

They were a raucous group as they entered through those pearly gates this first day of the reunion. There was John H. Miller, Thomas J. Mullady, Daniel Murphy, and William Nugent, just some of the boys from Brooklyn who when they partied it up let everyone in earshot know that a party meant everyone was supposed to be having a good time. Edmund L. Palen just smiled as he took in the scenario. How does one actually put into words what it is like to see all those friends who were taken from you a century ago in the prime of their youth?

Michael J. Regan and Malcolm T. Robertson danced the Irish jig Myles Sweeney had taught them their first day in the barracks at boot camp. "We still got it, Sweetie!" they called out to him using the nickname they had christened him with after the day Myles had shared with them a letter from his wife back in Brooklyn informing him he was a new daddy. She had signed it, "I love you so much, sweetie, looking forward to your safe return." In the world of male youths barely out of adolescence, that's all it took to earn a nickname that would follow you the rest of your life, even to heaven!

Frederick Young was never more excited to see all his New York friends again. He was one of the few members of the regiment not native to the Empire State, having come from Detroit, Michigan. It hadn't taken very long though for the rest of the boys to accept him as one of their own.

Walking toward the celebration were the two men the boys of the 69th had come to love more than anyone else in their lives save their wives and children. Joyce Kilmer and Father Francis Duffy walked in step with their arms around each other's shoulders. Seeing them first, Frank McMullin shouted out with great authority in his voice, "There they are, boys! There they are!"

In a great lunge of humanity the members of the regiment swarmed the beloved duo. Neither of them could stop the emotionally charged flock from lifting each of them upon their shoulders as they let out loud cheers of appreciation. They loved Joyce because of his ability to use words the way he did that expressed how they had all felt about one another. His poems about life had given them solace and comfort while they endured the boredom of existence in the trenches between the battles. Joyce had honored them, their sacrifices and their memories, with poems such as "Rouge Bouquet." He had put into words the emotions they were feeling but weren't able to express as clearly as Joyce could when he put his thoughts to paper.

On July 30, 1918, Joyce was killed during the Second Battle of the Marne. A sniper's bullet shattered that magnificent brain which had been appreciated by its proprietor as a gift from God and was used throughout his life in good stewardship as an acknowledgement for the blessing. The men cried unabashedly upon hearing the news of his demise; not only had they lost a friend and a brother, when Joyce died, a part of their lives had been taken away as well.

Their love for Father Francis Duffy was just as passionate. In many ways the good Father was more than a spiritual guide and comfort for the boys as they transitioned from training camp in the states to the battlefields of Europe where they evolved into men of integrity and character. He listened to them as they told him how hard it was to be away from family and loved ones. He gave them guidance on how to maintain their decency as humans in the face of great despair, especially in mourning the death of a friend at the front. He listened to their confessions as they examined their souls in attempts at reconciliation in an effort to make themselves pure in the eyes of God as they carried out the ungodly work of killing their fellow humans of the opposing army. He loved them and they knew it. Numerous times Father Duffy retrieved numbers of them from the battlefield in the face of enemy fire in order to provide them with medical care. They had seen him too many times during their stay in France offer up last rites over a fallen member of the regiment, tears slowly rolling down his strong features as he earnestly carried out God's work on earth. For some of the boys in the regiment who had grown up as orphans, Francis Duffy was their surrogate father, not just their religious guide in life.

When they exhausted themselves from passing around the gentlemen of their affection and allowed them once again to stand on the lush green grass of heaven's fields, Father Duffy took a few moments to regain control of his own emotions then solemnly asked all present to join him on bended knee in prayer and gratitude for the glory which was upon them.

United as one voice, they spoke the words which Father Duffy had prayed with them in the face of every adverse situation they had encountered during their time together in the 69th.

> *The Lord is my shepherd; I shall not want.*
> *He maketh me to lie down in green pastures:*
> *he leadth me beside the still waters.*
> *He restoreth my soul: he leadth me in the paths*
> *of righteousness for his name's sake.*

Yea, though I walk through the valley of the shadow of death, I will fear no evil: for thou art with me; thy rod and thy staff they comfort me.

Thou preparest a table before me in the presence of mine enemies: thou anointest my head with oil; my cup runneth over.

Surely goodness and mercy shall follow me all the days of my life: and I will dwell in the house of the Lord forever.

The words faded into heaven's skies.

A moment of dignified reflection followed as if everyone was soaking in the reality of the situation.

"And I will dwell in the house of the Lord forever," Father Duffy's voice alone boomed one more time. The smile on his face was easily noticeable even to those who were dozens of rows back from where Joyce and Father Duffy were standing. Every one of the 69th doughboys felt as if Father Duffy were looking straight into their eyes and talking directly to each of them as he added one more comment: "We are home, boys. God's plan for us has been fulfilled."

The whooping and applause and whistling along with the clapping and stomping of feet was so thunderous people in other parts of heaven at first thought a storm was brewing. They soon realized as everyone was experiencing that day that that deafening echo was that of another extraordinary group of people celebrating their long-awaited homecoming. What they did prove, however, was that even in heaven no one was more rambunctious or louder than New Yorkers.

18

"The incessant noise beat your eardrums into submission and after a while you actually became numb to the pounding and the throbbing. Your body quivered like it did when you had the chills and you couldn't much control that either but like most everything else that you experienced at the front you got used to that also, at least that was the lie you told yourself. At some point the artillery barrage would end. The shrill cry of someone just getting shot would instantly fade. The moaning of a wounded soldier who was bleeding to death in No Man's Land might linger for hours until the medical orderlies reached him and brought him back to our lines, or else he expired all alone while thousands of soldiers on both sides of the line did nothing to try and save him. At some point in time you could turn away from those sights and sounds, but what you could never evade as long as you were at the front was the smell of war."

Tears welled up in his eyes as he sat there replaying the horrors of his youth. One of the shepherds who had been tending his flock at the edge of the lush, green pasture had laid his staff down on the ground and was now quietly sitting next to him. Members of the flock baaed in the background aimlessly wandering around the idyllic scene. The shepherd held the young soldier's hand and quietly nodded his head as a sign for him to continue. The lad of twenty cleared the moisture which had blurred his vision. He continued to let his feelings flow forth.

"When it rained everything turned to mud, like a cesspool. It was a damp mildew odor that entered your nose and it seeped into your head and occupied your brain. Once it was there it never left, it just metastasized from one incessant aroma to another. Body sweat mixed with it and it attached to the inner part of your nostrils like crud that couldn't be removed. I never thought I could go a whole month without washing my body. I never knew that I would be able to tell someone what it actually felt like to be dirt. But the smell that seared itself into your brain was death. It was putrid. It was a sweet, disgusting aroma. Bodies that had been ripped open by shards of metal just oozed forth liquids of an array of tints and shades. Blood, water, guts, intestines, brains . . . white, red, gray, green . . . it was a whirlpool of desecration of the human body and spirit. It turned your stomach even if you looked away from the sight and you retched out your insides over your own uniform and boots."

He took a deep breath to compose his thoughts. He arched his head back and massaged his soft black hair with the palms of his hands. "That's the first time I've ever talked about it," he said while looking up into the sky. "My whole life, almost sixty years after the war, I could never find a way to talk about it. There never seemed to be a right moment to bring it up in polite conversation."

He sniffled back some of the emotion that was getting the best of him, but it was only a momentary victory. He shuddered and the tear ducts opened. "How do you explain to someone what it's like to smell death everyday of your life? How do you get someone to understand something that you can't understand yourself?" He coughed, clearing his throat while he cleared his eyes with a quick swipe of the back of his hand. "At night I'd dream about those bodies that littered the landscape and sucked the fresh air away from those who remained among the living. In the morning, or at dinner, or anytime that my nose inhaled the pleasure of fresh cooked food it would be overturned by the battle between my senses and my mind which could only comprehend burned human flesh rather than fresh bacon or a newly baked cake. It was always the smell of death, of bodies decomposing in the summer heat while flies and maggots celebrated their life cycle, of young men and boys whose bodies were cremated by shells in front of our eyes and denied the respect and decency of a formal burial."

Uncontrollable emotions ended his soliloquy, except for one last lament as he buried his face into his hands.

"It was all so ugly."

The shepherd remained mute, allowing him at his leisure additional time to conclude his emotional forthcoming as well as time to master his composure. Softly and with respectful empathy, he offered him cold water from his goat skin bottle. As the young soldier imbibed, it made his lips taste fresh. He could feel the pleasure roll over his tongue, slide down his throat, and course through his body. It made him feel new. In body and mind he was purified. His eyes remained closed as he savored the experience.

"The kingdom of heaven is yours," said the Good Shepherd in a peaceful and loving tone.

The young soldier, with the joys of eternal life imbued in his spirit, opened his eyes to behold a world he had once held so dear, and could now enjoy always. The memories of war, as well as the smells of war, were absent. The valley of the shepherd in which he had been sitting while sobbing and lamenting seemed to rise up and grasp his senses as if they had never before been utilized. The richness of the green in the majestic pines that dotted the hillsides emitted a scent of pleasure that took him back to childhood yuletides where life was innocent and filled with wonder. The fields of tall emerald grass allowed him to soak in the freshness of nature. The reassuring warmth of the sun's rays gently brushed against his face, now void of tears. The gentle scent of lilacs mixed with the loving aroma of roses which covered acre upon acre of the valley. He could feel his lungs expand and suck in the glory of life.

It was beautiful, and it would remain so forever.

19

"John Samuel Williams."

"John Thomas Williams."

"Timothy Aaron Williams."

"Timothy Abel Wilson."

"Anthony Warren Young."

"Peter Michael Young."

"Preston Andrew Yancey."

"Matthew Richard Zynkiewicz."

"Stanley Jonathan Zyziewicz."

Anita Ryerson took a soothing drawl of water from the fountain that trickled forth an infinite reservoir of cool, refreshing water. She had been patiently calling out the names of those she was looking for, hoping to meet at least a few of the more than one thousand names that were on the lists she had been reading from for going on a few hours. In the midst of millions of individuals as well as a like number of reunions among friends and family members, Anita knew her hopes of meeting anyone on her lists was small indeed, but this being heaven, a place where miracles were coming true, she persevered.

Fact was Anita was not related to any of the people she was looking for, at least that she knew about. Just as well, she had never met any of the individuals either. They were in heaven, at least for the moment, names on a list, just as they had been on earth during the war. Anita had spent a good part of the last year of the war working for the United States government in an office responsible for writing letters to parents and families informing them of the demise of their husbands, brothers and sons.

In some ways it was a job suitable for her at that moment in her life. She had suffered an injury working in the ammunition plants that prevented her from standing long periods of time. Sitting at a desk typing letters would be less physically demanding. It was a job that didn't require a lot of interaction between those who filled the office. Her quiet introverted demeanor was a result of a life time of hardship. Her parents had both died when she was a small child in an automobile accident and she was raised by numerous people in an orphanage until she turned eighteen. She had no siblings that she knew about. She was one of those people on earth who number in the millions but so often remain unknown to most other people.

While she basically remained unloved by others, she developed a quiet inner desire to care for others regardless of who they were. A silent empathy developed for those families she had never met but only knew through writing their addresses on an envelope and heading a letter that brought devastating news to each Mr. and Mrs. she typed onto the official light tan parchment style paper utilized as official government stationary. For Anita, each name of a soldier she wrote down was the name of a young man who, in a better life, could have been her brother, or in a happier life, her beau or eventual husband. Since she had known loss and pain much of her life, she had developed a genuine compassion for the individuals who had died somewhere in Europe or on the Atlantic Ocean, perhaps the victim of a U-boat attack or some other gruesome war-related accident.

Shortly after the war ended, Anita became ill with the influenza and similar to those vast numbers who succumbed to its destructive grasp, she also passed away, just as much a victim of the war as the other millions of her beleaguered generation.

As Anita began her task of calling out names again, starting all over with Allan Aames, she was quietly interrupted by St. Anthony, who had come up behind her without her knowledge of his presence. A gentle finger tap on her shoulder ceased her name announcements.

Upon making eye contact with the patron of lost causes, Anita could feel a surge of anticipatory joy vibrate throughout her being.

"In your earthly life, no one is truly ever alone. In our heavenly home, we are all one body, meaning family. Your rewards for your love of those lost ones will be forever enjoyed." As he finished speaking, he motioned with a rising motion of his head to a trio of young men who had appeared before Anita without her recognition.

"I am Anthony Warren Young," the lad not yet twenty spoke with a cheeriness that made Anita feel warm with appreciation.

"I am Peter Michael Young," said the duplicate standing next to Anthony. Not only were their physical features identical but the reverberations of their voices as well. "We wanted to thank you for your kindness toward our parents."

Excitement overcame her in a gusher of emotions. "You were the first two who I processed!" she said between a smile and tears starting to cover her cheeks. They hugged as a trio. The strength of their arms around her made her feel loved. It was a new experience.

Their embrace loosened and each took a step back in order to converse with one another.

"My first day on the job," Anita began talking with them as if they had been friends she had known all her life, "I had just sat down at my desk and started to read the information about you, Anthony. It said you were killed somewhere in the Argonne Forest from heavy artillery fire. I started to cry but quietly so no one else in the office would think I couldn't do the job. I remember reading the word 'forest' and thinking you must have been all alone when you were killed and how sad that was for something to happen like that."

Anthony smiled sheepishly. "Truth is, I don't remember how many were with me when that shell landed among us. I just remember the pain that seared through my body in such a short time and then nothing. Dead, just like that."

Anita matched eyes with Peter, the younger of the two by six minutes but the second one to die that particular day. "Your letter was next, and I after I read it, it took me a little while to realize that you were brothers. I don't think I ever put it together you were twins.

Anyway my hands began trembling at how awful that was going to be for your parents when they received the news."

Peter stepped forward and hugged Anita a second time while Anthony rubbed his eyes to control his emotions.

"We know about the other letters, Anita," Anthony said quietly. "We wanted to make sure we found you up here to say thank you."

Anita blushed. "They were just formal letters, that's all. The government told us what to write and we typed it out on the form. Everyone got the same kind of notices about the death of a family member."

Anthony and Peter winked at each other as two kids might do in keeping a secret from their elders.

"You know which letters we mean, Anita. The personal ones you wrote to our parents. We met Mom and Dad earlier and one of the things that they talked about were your letters, the ones you wrote to them concerning each one of our deaths."

"It meant so much to them knowing that someone took the time to communicate with them about their children," added Peter. "Our mom especially said you must be some kind of exceptional individual to have taken time to try and make complete strangers feel a little better about something so horrendous in their lives."

Anita smiled shyly. "I never had anyone special in my life. When I read those two letters about your deaths it was the first time in my life I realized that someone else must be worse off than I could ever be. I quit feeling sorry for myself that day and I decided I would try to help someone who had a real problem or crisis compared to mine."

"Our father said he read your letters on more than one occasion as a way of trying to understand our deaths. He questioned a lot how it was that both of us were killed on the same day. Maybe it had something to do with us being born on the same day and all, but he could never figure it out to his satisfaction." Peter paused. "Your letters helped him appreciate that care and love existed in a world that was filled with war and hatred. Each time he read them it helped him let go of the anger he experienced at our dying."

Anthony reached out to hold Anita's hands in his. "When you wrote that you would pray for our souls as well as to ask God that He help soothe the pain our parents would be experiencing upon news of our deaths, our dad and our mom told us that they would begin praying for others who had experienced the same loss as they had. You convinced them that humanity and love were not destroyed by the war."

"It helped them endure the years after the war, until they passed sometime in the 1950s," added Peter with a tone of appreciation.

"I thank both of you for your kind words," Anita responded to their praise, not sure what else to say.

Anthony now wrapped one arm around Anita and held her closer. "Did you really write a personal letter to each family that you sent an official death notification?" he admiringly inquired.

"Yes, I did," Anita stated with a newfound sense of sureness in her voice. "All told, I believe it was 1,011. What you are telling me now makes me surely realize how important it was that I did what I did."

"Do you remember writing a letter to a Miss Julie Anne Wilkins about the death of Timothy Abel Wilson?"

Peter watched as Anita's brow crinkled in thought. It was as though she was mentally re-reading all those notices which crossed her desk that last year of the war.

"Yes, I do," Anita said decisively. "My first thought was why they didn't share the same last name. I thought it must have been due to a divorce or something like that."

"It's a little more complicated than that," injected the solemn tone of St. Anthony, who had been watching the previous event unfold while sitting quietly with the third soldier who had accompanied the Young brothers.

"Julie Anne Wilkins adopted Timothy Abel Wilson when he was just a newborn. He had come from the McKee Orphanage in Baltimore, Maryland." Upon hearing the name of the orphanage where she had been placed as a child, Anita's eyes widened. St. Anthony noticed her reaction but continued his tale with the same control of emotion he used to initiate the conversation. "Timothy had been left at the orphanage with a baby sister, who would be you. There are no records of who your parents were."

Anita brushed past St. Anthony and for the first time paid attention to the quiet soldier who now was just smiling at her. The crinkle in his nose and the way his jaw presented itself she knew as that which had stared back at her anytime in her life she had looked into a mirror or viewed a photograph of herself.

"Hi, sister," he said in a kind, peaceful tone, "I only found out a short while ago. You might not remember when you read about my death during the war, but I was one of those men killed along with the shell blast that killed Anthony."

Anita embraced him and their arms squeezed one another with a feeling of love that seemed to release a lifetime of pent-up emotion that neither had been able to somehow share with anybody else throughout their mortal lives. It was as though they had always felt that something was missing in their lives but they could never fully explain what it was.

As some might say upon reviewing this tale, regardless of how clichéd it might sound, it was a reunion made in heaven.

20

They were married for fifty-two years and died within two days of one another. They were married three years to the day after first seeing one another on Christmas Eve in 1893 at a midnight mass in their local parish where they had grown up as kids. Their only son, Robert, was born in 1897. They lost him in 1915, a casualty of the Loos offensive. He was one of fifty thousand casualties which would soon be replaced by a new wave of young soldiers who would be sent to their deaths the following year. As previously stated, however, he was the only son of Winston and Victoria MacDonald. Robbie was their only offspring and family pride who was supposed to carry on the family heritage.

They received a home-delivered telegram in the middle of a beautiful autumn afternoon while they were out in the garden tending to some flowers which would be deceased in a few weeks due to the change in weather. Perhaps it was a harbinger that they should have observed more keenly, but as parents dealing with the everyday stress of having their only son in the thick of the fighting on the continent, they had agreed among themselves that it was best to never talk about the war unless they received a letter from Robert. Only then, with a letter in their hand and proof that he was alive, would they sit down at breakfast over tea and toast with blackberry jam made from their garden harvest would they allow themselves to express their views to one another about what the war was doing to them.

The telegram was indecisive, at least in their minds. Robert was not dead. He was not a prisoner of war. He was not wounded. A new category that many parents and family were starting to get acquainted with throughout Great Britain was the term "missing." After the mail courier carried out his responsibility and departed their premises, Winston and Victoria sat side by side alone with their thoughts an extended period of time before either one vocalized a view.

"I guess if he is just missing he will be found in due time," Victoria said. "At least he is alive and not hurt."

"I don't understand how they can just lose track of him," Winston offered, naïve to the realities of modern war. It didn't help any either that the government was doing a masterful job of keeping the realities of war sanitized for the benefit of the public and families of casualties in particular.

No one wanted to be informed that their loved one was blasted into smithereens by howitzer shells that were big enough to sink warships. No one wanted to face the fact that machine guns that could discharge thousands of rounds a minute could shred identifiable body features to look like ground chuck. There was a reason the soldiers themselves used the phrase "the meat grinder" to refer to areas of the battlefield that were scenes of indiscriminate slaughter. The carnage could not be exaggerated. The truth would make most civilians regurgitate their stomach contents in seconds if they ever saw the real photographs or films of those killed in action. "Missing" usually meant that the soldier in question was dead but the authorities could not locate the body or positively identify the deceased so they had no other option than to use the term. It was a new reality of war that would affect thousands and thousands of families from every belligerent nation involved in the great global conflict.

Throughout the duration of the war, Winston and Victoria MacDonald would receive a telegram from the British Imperial War Office on a monthly or bimonthly basis regretfully informing them that the official status of Private Robert MacDonald had not changed. A day after the armistice was declared they received an updated status officially declaring Robbie as "missing and presumed dead." While they had spent the past few years mourning the loss of their son, they had clung on to the hope that he would be found in some hospital or German prison camp. To see the word "dead" associated with his name and status for the first time carried with it a sense of finality. Another fear that crept into their deteriorating mental psyche was if anyone in the government or army wanted to keep looking for their "missing and presumed dead" son now that the war was over.

While they slowly began to accept that Robbie was dead, especially with the end of hostilities, it was haunting not knowing where their flesh and blood was along with the mystery of how he died remaining unsolved as well. There was no sense of relief in any way when the telegram that came to their abode five years to the day of the armistice stating that Robbie was going to be officially declared "Dead, killed in military operations on the Western Front." It appeared that their worst fear had come true, and would be compounded the rest of their lives with the body of their child never being recovered or delivered back to them for a final viewing or a proper burial.

Their marriage lasted as long as it did because they needed each other to lean on as the years passed and neither of them could get over not knowing what happened to Robbie. It was a strange existence. They didn't eat a lot. Neither had an appetite that could overcome the stress and despair which reminded them daily of their sorrow. They set a plate for Robbie every time they set a table for themselves. Even as years turned into decades they carried out the same procedure with each meal. They even washed Robbie's clean plate and glass even though it was never soiled. As for celebrating holidays, they quit doing that within the first year of being notified that Robbie was missing. There just wasn't a desire to celebrate since there was no longer anything joyous in their life.

A few times their hopes were raised when news reports periodically talked about bodies of soldiers from the war being recovered by some French farmer while plowing their fields. In fact, the French government even had a whole bureaucratic institution in place after the war to retrieve and identify as many soldiers as possible who remained buried in the fields of France. However, none of those excavated bodies returned to England were Robbie.

As the years of their lives wore away, they realized they were not experiencing life but just existing. Not talking about Robbie contributed to them not talking about most things married couples would find to talk about on a daily basis. In their hearts they still very much loved one another but Winston and Victoria seemed to have an unspoken agreement not to bring up Robbie's name in any conversation for fear of making the other one hurt more than they were both already experiencing. When Winston would come across Victoria weeping or vice versa, the other would just sit down and hold their partner's hand until the mourning session ended.

Old age and a life of despair ended their lives within days of one another. It didn't seem right that the war haunted them until their dying days, but it was typical of the grasp the conflict retained on the generation who had gone off to war or supported the war with grand enthusiasm in the summer of 1914.

When the trumpets of the Grand Reunion summoned them for their entrance into heaven, they could hardly restrain their emotions. They walked in together holding hands, swinging them back and forth as they did in the early days of their lives when Robbie was still theirs to hold and treasure. They were directed by helpful and enthusiastic angels to an area called "The Saint Jude Plains." It was more like a giant field surrounded by a forest of firs which created a most lovely venue for a reunion of lost children from their parents.

Robbie came walking toward them out of the shade of the trees. His face was so clean and young looking. Not a trace of the earth which had concealed his body since that day in the war he went missing was to be seen anywhere on his body. He strode toward them with the vigor of youth, a swagger of life in his step. He was eighteen again, the whole prime of his life waiting to be experienced and enjoyed. Winton and Victoria had their stolen lives presented to them again as well. There would be no missing years here, only life everlasting. They hugged and they cried vociferously, gaining the attention of those nearby who were celebrating their own reunions with long lost loved ones. They also smiled. For the first time since 1918, they smiled.

21

The water brushed over his hair as he broke the calm surface of Lake Saint John the Baptist. The breath of life filled his nostrils with a cool sensation that filtered throughout his body, now renewed with the Holy Spirit of eternal life. The temperature of the lake was soothing and created an atmosphere of secure comfort, akin to being held in the arms of a dear loved one. The warmth on his face from the rays of the sun reinforced the safety perpetuated by the surrounding setting.

The smile on Isaac Fordwick's face was back. Not since the terror drowning that he experienced as a passenger on the *Lusitania* in 1915 had he been able to enjoy the joy of just being happy for no particular reason at all. Perhaps that is the way all seven-year-olds live their daily life, before the stresses of adulthood creep in and destroy that wonderment of innocence.

Like many of those killed at sea due to U-Boat attacks or combat with other naval vessels, Isaac's body was claimed by the sea, his remaining family members never being given a chance to have a proper burial for him. It was an emptiness felt by countless families of all combatant nations during The Great War. In a strange twist of fate, he had actually died with a number of his family members since they were traveling together on vacation aboard the majestic British liner under the false belief that as citizens of a neutral America at that time in the war, they were safe from any harm.

Isaac, his mother, Alice, and his older sister, Fiona, who was eleven, were at least able to die together. As the waters rose up and engulfed the ship in its last throes of life, Alice grasped Isaac's and Fiona's hands and the trio slipped under the hostile waters of the North Sea to their final earthly resting place. Matthew Fordwick, husband and father of the family, was not on the *Lusitania*, having stayed back in the United States to attend to business. Having survived the war, and living until he was seventy-nine, he passed away toward the end of the twentieth century, never being able to deal with the hollowness that comes with losing the loved ones which constitute the focus of one's life.

Now, here he was, in the glory of his younger days, laughing, swimming with his children and his beloved Alice. It was as though the tragedy of the *Lusitania* had never happened, and though they remembered the event it no longer occupied their minds. Heaven was sweeter than any tragic event which may at one time have consumed their existence.

"Catch me, Daddy," Fiona playfully challenged him after splashing him with a handful of water and then swimming away. His decision to swim after his beloved daughter was made harder by a new wave of water hitting the side of his head.

"No, catch me, Father," yelled Isaac with a whimsical tone in his voice.

Lying on her floating raft a few short feet away, Alice watched quietly as her husband and children frolicked in the soothing waters of the lake.

Like everything they would come to know that was good in heaven, the lake was endless. A quick scan in any direction showed countless numbers of people enjoying the elation of being a part of the grand reunion in their own ways. There was unencumbered room for everyone, with all able to enjoy private moments of glory with their loved ones in the midst of endless public encounters.

Alice caught sight of a lone individual on the shore, quite a distance away from her location. Though she couldn't identify who she was looking at, the body language of the snappy dresser in his all white uniform, topped with a high brimmed hat, gave the appearance that maybe there was one person here not enjoying themselves. She wondered if the unknown figure had not yet met their loved ones.

Alice's train of thought however was quickly broken as the playful hands of Matthew, Fiona, and Isaac soon began rocking her raft from side to side. Her focus shifted to the smiles of her loved ones who gave her no warning to prepare for being dumped into the water. She could hear their giggles and laughter as she slipped under the water after they had successfully upended the raft. It was like being on a picnic the way things were before the war was ever a thought in anybody's mind.

On the shore, the lone figure, no longer a concern of Alice, was now sitting along the water's edge with an occasional lap of the lake wetting his shoes. He paid no attention to the moistness which was now seeping through not only his fashionable footwear but his complimenting fine hosiery as well. At times the incoming water that hit a protruding rock sprayed his face with a spritz of coolness, but nothing seemed to break his deep train of thoughtfulness.

His name was Walther Schwieger. As a youngster, he dreamed of being on the sea, enjoying the freedom that would surely match his spirit of adventure. His path in life eventually led to him being captain of his own ship. With pride, Lieutenant Walter Schwieger of the German Imperial Navy of the Kaiser sailed off to war early in 1915 ready to defend the Fatherland.

As he sat along the lake's edge, he let his conscience dominate his mind. While he believed as all did that God didn't make mistakes, he arrived at the conclusion that he knew he didn't belong here with everyone else. He raised himself to his feet with the intention of seeking out someone who could help him comprehend his predicament. It was only then that he noticed that spongy sopping feeling within his shoes.

"Maybe you should kick them off, as well as those fine socks and just let the coolness of the fresh water relax your soul."

Walter raised his head out of his mental soliloquy and gazed into the eyes of the Lord.

"I knew you would be looking for me eventually," he said with a soft smile.

"I killed so many people," Walter whispered, barely audible. "Not just those on the *Lusitania*." He paused. "All together I sank forty-nine ships. All those sailors . . . I destroyed food and supplies that would have kept people alive . . ." His voice trailed off, choked with sobs.

"Sit back down again," the Lord motioned to him. "I sent my son into the world to save the sinners, not those who were false prophets and false leaders."

Walter bowed his head in shame.

"I killed helpless people. I was awarded medals. There is no grandeur in that." He raised his head and for the first time his eyes directly met those of his Lord. "Yours is the glory. The weakness of man does not deserve the wonders of heaven."

The Lord reached out and held Walter's hands. It comforted him.

"As your own ship was sinking in 1917, as the water cascaded into the hatch, as it rose up around you reaching to drown your life . . . at the hour of your death . . . do you remember your last words, Walter?"

His eyes opened wide in a moment of realization. His hands grasped his Lord's hands tighter.

"I said, 'Lord, have mercy on all those souls whose lives I have taken. I am sorry for my wicked actions.'"

The Lord smiled at him in that reassuring way that all loving fathers reassure their children that everything is going to be all right.

"Even as the cold waters of death stung at your body and flowed over your head, your thoughts and actions were those of contrition, as well as asking mercy for those who had perished at your hand."

A large splash of water clipped the side of Walter's face.

He didn't notice that the Good Shepherd had quietly moved on as Walter looked toward the source of the disruption. A large red play ball had landed close by causing the spray from the lake. Its owner was now coming into view to retrieve his toy. It was Isaac Fordwick, closely followed by his parents and sister.

"Sorry about that, Mister," the youngster apologized. "Would you like to join our family as we swim? My mom thought it would be nice to invite you to enjoy some time with us."

Walter could feel his body lighten as the anguish and apprehension he felt earlier had exited his vessel.

"I would love to join you," he responded with cheer as he turned toward Matthew and Alice offering them his hand. "My name is Walter Schw—"

"We know who you are, Mr. Schwieger," Matthew Fordwick said with a welcoming smile on his face and without a tone of cheeriness leaving his voice. "We are happy we can all be here together."

22

Behind home the catcher bobbed on his knees waiting for the pitch to be delivered. He straightened his wiry mask and pounded a fist into his mitt. He could feel jolts of strength shoot through his arms. Dust, which had accumulated from games of old and laid undisturbed for decades as the mitt sat on his bedroom shelf waiting for its owner to use it again, rose into the air enough for the rejuvenated protector of the plate to use his free hand to try and dissipate the quiet annoyance.

It was the little oddities and nuances associated with the game he missed the most. He had never paid attention to them until he had time to think about it while he lay in the hospital bed in France adjusting to his wounds for the first six months after the armistice was announced. In the trenches it wasn't the exciting dust kicked up by a sliding runner or the somewhat gentle residual of the umpire sweeping clean the pitcher's target between batters, it was mud, always mud, or so it seemed. After a heavy rain, you sank in it sometimes all the way up to your knees. The suction was so strong it pulled your boots off when you tried to extricate yourself from its gooey, squishy yet viselike grasp. It felt like hands reaching up from the underworld itself tightly grasped around your ankles pulling and yanking at your feet and legs not wanting to let you move in any direction. It was the situation he had been in when the German bombardment began.

He had watched as others to the side of him who shared the same muddy predicament were blasted to smithereens from direct hits. Mortar shells seemed to drop directly on top of the portion of the trench he and members of his platoon had been trying to traverse at that particular moment. The shell that took his hands landed close enough to him so that he thought he could retrieve the half-buried explosive canister from the mud and heave it out of the trench before it detonated. It erupted just as it rolled off the tips of his fingers, taking off both hands down to the elbows. His oversized steel helmet deflected some of the blast away from his face and when the rest of his body fell into the soupy mud, it staunched the flow of blood coming from the wounds of his lost limbs.

Medics and buddies were upon the scene in such a quick manner that they were able to extricate him from the muddy swirl before he suffocated, having fallen face forward and no longer capable of trying to save his own life. They poured water down his heat-seared face to remove the mud from his eyes, nose, and mouth and he lunged forward for a giant gasp of fresh air while at the same time he emitted particles of the soiled earth from his mouth. Once he was back in the hospital, procedures were started that would last up to half a year to try and save what was left of his arms. Eventually both would be amputated at the shoulder.

Having his arms and hands back the way they were before the war, in the days of his youth when the possibility of a professional baseball career loomed on the horizon of his life, made his whole body tingle with joy. To play the game he loved, the way he used to be able to do so before the war was what heaven was all about. His experience was similar to the innumerable numbers who suffered from a plethora of physical debilitating injuries inflicted upon them by the violence of the international idiocy many liked to refer to as "the Great War."

Short of death, there is nothing more depressing than seeing a young athlete have their prowess snatched from them in the prime of their life.

The fading dust residue reached his nostrils and as it penetrated his senses he relished being able to play the game he loved. His youth returned, he was whole again. The simple grin he couldn't hold back broke into a wholesome smile of joyful innocence as he peered toward pitcher's mound.

His battery mate stood there soaking in the experience as well. The freshness of the air rejuvenated his scarred and worn-out lungs. During the war, Christy Mathewson was on the receiving end of a dose of poison gas. Even though he returned to play major league baseball after the war with the New York Giants, he was never the same physically as he was before the war. Now, with each deep breath of fresh air, he could feel the vigor of youth course through his body. His muscles felt taut and strong even before he put them into play. The old leather glove on one hand and his fingers working their way around the baseball in the other as he felt for the most advantageous way to grasp it before he delivered it all felt so natural to him.

Walking up to the plate . . . yes, *walking* up to the plate was a twenty-year-old Iowan who earlier in the day when he first saw the heavenly field thought he was back home near his farm and cornfield where he had played so many ball games on a field laid out by his dad. He had had both of his legs shredded by shrapnel during the American offensive in Belleau Wood. One had been sheared off at the knee on the battlefield and the other was amputated above the knee a few hours later that same day at a field hospital. The jubilation of walking to the plate was so overwhelming that it took him a few moments to realize why the umpire, catcher, and pitcher were all grinning at him and the pleasurable refrain, "Play ball!" had *not* been bellowed. He hadn't brought a bat with him from the dugout.

Everyone enjoyed the moment as he sheepishly bounded back to retrieve one of his smooth wooden favorites. Standing back in the batter's box, he waited for the challenge from Mathewson to become a reality. The ball came in high at chest level, just where he liked it. His swing was majestic and he could feel the muscles in his legs give him the strength to drive the ball deep to center field, but only if he had hit it. The ball had dipped just as he swung and was now safely embedded in the soft, dusty leather of the catcher's mitt.

"Strike one!" announced the umpire with as much glee in his voice comparable to the feelings everyone else was experiencing during their first game in God's Backyard Fields. His vocal cords were back at full strength, no longer strained and nearly muted as the phosgene gas had left them from 1918 until his death as a quiet, bitter old man in 1992.

The next pitch followed the same flight path as the previous pitch, but this time instead of swinging, he guided his bat forward and softly redirected the ball down the third base line. Coming out of the left side of the batter's box, he could already feel the speed building up in his legs as he began the race down the first base line. The battery mates charged from their positions, one with the quickness of a panther, the other with the stealth of a cheetah. The young catcher reached the bunt first and twirled around to place a perfect strike into the waiting mitt of the first basemen. He had stretched out as much as physically possible without taking his back leg off of the base, and presenting his teammate as close a target as can be in order to get the runner out.

The ball thudded into the first basemen's glove with accuracy and authority but half a second too late as the batter reached the bag safely legging out an infield hit.

The play was over but the beauty of the scene was realized and appreciated by all of those who witnessed it, and especially by those who had participated in it.

Christy stared at the runner who now stood safely on first. He had been outwitted on the play, and he could appreciate that. While he mulled over how he would pitch to the next batter, he was also aware of how refreshing it was to have been able to run again without any irritation or pain thumping forth from his lungs.

The catcher crouched back down behind the plate, a little upset that his throw did not beat the runner, but more than satisfied at having had the pleasure once again to leap forward, retrieve the ball with his hands, his wonderful hands, and throw it.

The first baseman banged his glove off his thigh as he settled in to hold the runner on the bag. It was his first game of baseball since he had been killed in 1918.

The runner stood there quietly letting his body talk to him. The adrenaline had not subsided. Rivulets of sweat ran down his neck. His heart thumped in excitement and happiness. He could feel his leg muscles still quivering in the aftermath of the hard run from home to first and then some as he had continued down the line after touching the bag.

It was all they had been waiting for, to enjoy again the simple game of a time that once had them believing that they would be forever young . . . and here in heaven, not Iowa as some, at first, believed it to be, it was all true.

23

The young, sandy-haired lad of eighteen sat on the soft grass of the hillside surrounded by six nurses. The youngest of them, sitting in front and to the side of him, looked back over her shoulder and flashed the same reassuring smile she had shown him during the last seven years of his life that she had cared for him at the veteran's nursing home. "I always told you that you would see your pals again," she happily reminded him.

A soft smile broke across his face. For the first time, all of the nurses who had cared for him throughout his life in his post-war world were gathered together. Each in their own kind way had shown him the resolve and love that was needed in trying to care for someone who could never understand the guilt of living as well as the loss of beloved friends he mourned on a daily basis for close to seventy years before truly passing away from a broken heart.

"Thank you, Alice. You were always so patient with me," he responded with the most sincere gratitude in his voice. In silence he tried to calculate how many times a day, a week, a month, over the course of more than six decades, that he had gently asked his attending nurse on a given day, "When will I see my pals again?"

Since that July 1st morning in 1916 when he and his pals went over the top and into No Man's Land to be slaughtered whole companies at a time in the face of withering German machine gun fire, Sebastian Blake was consumed with the thought of seeing his friends and comrades once again. Whereas the close to twenty thousand killed that day, the flower of Britain's youth in the third year of the war, were eventually retrieved and buried under the earth which they had previously trod forth upon, and the near forty thousand wounded were rounded up and cared for as best as physicians could do in the early parts of the twentieth century, Sebastian had survived that day, unscathed in the physical realm.

Historians rarely, if ever, turned their focus or thoughts on the survivors of the first day of the Battle of the Somme. The wholesale mechanized butchering of thousands and thousands of young men in the prime of their youth, on one day, within a matter of hours, understandably has led to most people not just forgetting about those who survived that day, but not even thinking about them in the first place.

Sebastian Blake was a member of the Accrington Pals, one of the units established early in the war when the British government encouraged friends and neighbors of whole towns and communities to sign up together so they could go off to war together, defeat the German Hun together, and earn medals and eternal glory together for King and Country. No one ever imagined them dying together in such overwhelming, mind-numbing quantities.

The Accrington Pals were formed by enthusiastic volunteers from the town of Accrington in Lancashire as well as the neighboring towns of Burnley, Blackburn, and Chorley. Together they would become known in the British military as the 11th Battalion of the East Lancashire Regiment. In the negligent enthusiasm whipped up by government-formulated nationalism, no one of age, or near age, for that matter, wanted to be left out of going to France to crush the armies of the evildoer Kaiser. Sebastian would not only join up with his best friends and classmates Jonathan Wilmot, Edward Middleton, Brian Archbald, Kenneth Wellington, Thomas Masterson, and Riley Alister Kinkaid, but he would be able to enjoy the rewards of becoming heroes with his pals, something they could savor the rest of their lives at regimental reunions as they aged together into the twilight of their years.

As they ascended the trenches all of their romantic images of war blew up in their faces. Ahead of him on the ladder he would climb on his first step to martial glory was Jonathan Wilmot, Sebastian's next door neighbor and friend since the day they were born a few hours apart back on a sunny August morning in 1897. Blood spurted out the back of Jonathan's head from two holes created by well-placed machine gun rounds before the rest of his body was able to rise out of the trench and advance into No Man's Land. As Sebastian rubbed his friend's blood and brains off of his face, he could feel the weight of the deceased bounce off his head and shoulders as it continued its backward and downward descent into the depths of the trench.

As the evolution of the battle continued, Sebastian could feel the hands of soldiers from behind pushing him upward on the ladder accompanied by sharp commands of "Keep your ass moving," and "Go forward, go forward." Adrenaline mixed with fear helped him make it out of the trench. He progressed less than twenty yards before seeing Edward Middleton's body being pierced repeatedly with bullets. He saw Edward's head snap back as his friend's chest seemed to explode into little geysers of blood as shot after shot pummeled the life out of him. For some reason he would never understand, Sebastian noticed that while Edward's helmet had been knocked off of his head, his glasses remained snug around each earlobe. So many bullet holes had shredded his ribs and chest that Sebastian couldn't count them all as he progressed past his second dead friend.

Proceeding, he could see Brian Archbald and Kenneth Wellington keeping pace of one another about a yard in front of him and two yards to his left. His vision blurred for a second as drips of sweat made their way from under his helmet down his forehead and into his eyes. He blinked and squeezed his eyelids in a quick attempt to rid himself of the annoyance. In that proverbial blink of an eye, two more of his pals died. He passed them as both seemed to fall simultaneously as the German machine gunners continued the butchering of Britain's youth. He was close enough to both of them to hear the hard thudding impact of machine gun bullets striking their uniforms on their way to entering their bodies and releasing them from their earthly existence.

Blood splatter sprayed the left side of his face mixing with the perspiration that continued to effuse itself from his body. Sebastian's foot tripped over a rock protruding haphazardly from the battlefield and as his knee buckled and he began to tumble forward multiple shell blasts from the German trench mortars erupted in front of him. The combined force of the blasts was so powerful that they stopped his forward falling motion and propelled his body backward a whole five yards. He slammed into the ground back first and lay there slightly concussed and stunned looking up into the smoke-covered sky that quietly looked down upon him and the sadness that was the attack.

Barely a second later, the strong, caring hands of his pals Thomas Masterson and Riley Alister Kincaid were reaching toward him to pull him back to his feet. Unknown to Sebastian, they had been behind him since they left the trench and had seen him go down. He saw their smiles as each one of them grasped an arm of his and initiated his ascension back to his feet. From violent confusion and relentless terror his emotions quickly switched to one of safety and comfort as his pals momentarily restricted their advance forward in order to assist him.

The whirlwind of emotions continued as fear reentered Sebastian's body. His body was halfway to erect when the fulcrums of strength that had just assuaged his feelings crumpled on either side of him. He saw Riley's legs buckle while Thomas grunted out in a subdued moan as blood shot forth from his mouth onto Sebastian's uniform. With no one pulling him upward as his dead pals fell toward him, Sebastian fell in reverse, once again landing on his back. He was covered by Riley's body first and the extra weight which crushed down on them as he lay there registered in his mind that Thomas had finished his fall as well. He wriggled his body a little to try and escape from underneath of them but the weight of his pack still attached to his back, and the combined poundage of his two pals who now lay on top of him, did not allow for him to push them off of him or slide out from underneath of them.

His physical condition and his mental condition intertwined. He was still woozy from the first shell blast he had experienced and the adrenaline rush from the time he left the trenches to this moment, a grand total of no more than five minutes at best, was over. He was beginning to feel the throbbing inside his skull. Perspiration and blood, his and Riley's, dripped down the side of his face. He felt pain in his legs but didn't know the source of it. His right arm was lying across his chest pinned in an awkward position by the bodies of his deceased pals. He tried to move it but it just didn't seem to work. There was no energy or power in it. He left arm, exposed and free from the human entanglement of the trio, didn't possess enough strength or energy to assist in any attempt to extricate himself from his fate. His mind relayed to him the message that nothing could be done. With total exhaustion now conquering his body, Sebastian closed his eyes. Within seconds his world blacked out.

Around him, the murder of the Pals battalions continued unabated.

24

The day ended with 584 of 720 members of the 11th Battalion of the East Lancashire Regiment being killed or wounded.

Eighteen-year-old Sebastian Blake lost all six of his pals. They were his hometown friends since he was a little boy, and in the case of Jonathan Wilmot, from the day he was born. They were all dead, killed within a span of five minutes. Adding to the tragedy was that he witnessed each of them being murdered.

A few hours after the fighting abated, stretcher bearers came upon the trio of friends stacked on top of each other. By that point in time, Riley's blood soaked face had been resting against Sebastian's cheek and once the orderlies were aware that Sebastian was still alive, they took care to break the physical connection which had ensued due to the blood drying and caking up over the hours of the warm summer day. A young private no older than Sebastian gently poured some water on the spot where Riley's and Sebastian's skin was fused together in order to make the blood moist again. With the soft touch of an adoring angel he slid Riley's head to the side and they were free. Two other orderlies then placed Riley's body on a stretcher and began their walk with him to the rear where they were lining up the dead in order to ascertain an exact count of the day's casualties, and hopefully make identification of the deceased in order to notify the next of kin back in Britain.

It would eventually be determined that 19,240 men, many of them still boys, died that July 1st. Another 38,230 were wounded.

Sebastian slowly rose to his feet. He watched quietly as the cleaners of the battlefield placed a sheet across Thomas Masterson's face and then followed in the footsteps of those who had previously removed Riley Alister Kincaid's body. A wave of anxiety ran through Sebastian and he quickly spun around to look behind him in order to see the bodies of Jonathan Wilmot, Edward Middleton, Brian Archbald, and Kenneth Wellington one last time but it was too late. Their dead, decimated bodies had already been removed from the battlefield. His stomach began to feel filled and his legs quivered. He dropped to his knees and vomited. The young orderly came running back to assist him up to his feet but Sebastian was empty. His spirit was withered. His will was gone. He remained on his knees and his head sagged as though it were no longer connected to his spine.

The orderly gingerly placed a hand on Sebastian's shoulder in a vain attempt to offer some sort of empathy, but in fairness to the young lad who had been collecting the dead and wounded for countless hours, his experience was making him numb to the sights he was encountering. The reality was that he didn't know what to say to Sebastian or any of the other young, disillusioned survivors he encountered while he carried out his responsibilities. Feeling the pressure of the slight touch the orderly placed upon his shoulder, Sebastian belatedly raised his head just enough to look into the young boy's eyes and quietly ask him, "When will I see my pals again?"

Those were the only words Sebastian would say the rest of his days on earth. They diagnosed him with severe shell shock once he was assisted from the battlefield and looked at by empathetic doctors who had no cure for what the dark side of humanity had done to him.

During the first few weeks that he was under army supervision and medical care, they asked him question after question trying to figure out a way to get Sebastian to communicate with them. "Who were your pals? What were their last names? What were their first names? Did you see your pals get killed? What do you remember about the battle?"

Sebastian never responded to any of the questions. In the mornings when he woke up, it was noted by nurses who kept watch of the wounded throughout the ward that catered to shell shock victims, Sebastian had slept peacefully. He never talked in his sleep, he never woke up screaming or in a cold sweat, shaking all over, he never acted out toward an orderly, he never tried to hurt himself in a fit of self remorse, he never did anything other than ask in the same quiet tone he did that day back on the Somme battlefield, "When will I see my pals again?"

When asked what he wanted for breakfast, lunch, and dinner, he responded by quietly asking, "When will I see my pals again?" His expression never changed. All of the doctors or nurses who attended to him over the entirety of his life noted in their reports and remarks that the "patient shows no emotion," or "the patient shows no outward signs of expression," or "the patient remains mute except to inquire about his pals."

Now, sitting on one of heaven's silky grass hillsides watching those who had been killed at the Battle of the Somme pass in front of him as on the barracks review fields of old, Sebastian could feel his heart pumping with the joys of anticipation, like a child moments before coming around the corner of the room on Christmas morning to encounter a pile of presents under the great green pine decorated in all of its glory, waiting for him to enjoy.

And just like that, there they were.

They were six abreast. Jonathan Wilmot was on the near left. Next to him and then down the line were Edward Middleton, Brian Archbald, Kenneth Wellington, Thomas Masterson, and Riley Alistar Kincaid. They walked in sync with arms linked. Great gushing smiles highlighted the beautiful youthful features of their faces.

"There are my pals, Alice!" Sebastian shouted with such enthusiasm that even in heaven where highly emotional reunions by the millions were taking place, the intensity put forth from his vocal cords sent an additional shiver of happiness through everyone who heard him. The love he had kept bottled within for the last sixty plus years of his life led to uncontrollable emotions as the pals embraced as one. Sebastian could barely see them with all the tears obfuscating his vision. That mattered little since he could hear their voices shouting his name with unabated glee as well as feel the warmth of their hugs and back slaps.

The emotions on display of the pals associated with the Battle of the Somme were so overwhelming that the flow of those entering through heaven's gates was slowed so much that in Earth time it would take two full days for all of them to enter into God's realm.

25

Near one of the meadows a short distance beyond where the Somme celebrations were occurring, a more serene scene was playing out. The black-haired, frail soldier in his mid-twenties sat alone on a plush patch of wavy light green grass with his back resting comfortably against a large rock. He shared the moment with his puppy, a small white terrier that playfully tried to lick his fingers each time he went to stroke her head.

He had had few friends at the front and those he did were killed in action in the early years of the conflict. While he had entered the war eager to serve his country, and his passion for his homeland never wavered, he spent most of his off duty time in mental isolation, and silently brooded about the death of his beloved mother a few years before the war. From the moment she passed beyond earth's realm, he had always felt alone even in the company of others. He enjoyed the solace of spending time with his pet. It was the only time he felt mutual unconditional love. Sometimes it seemed the only one who understood his angst and sadness was the puppy he cupped gently in his forearm and lovingly caressed for hours with his free hand. The war had eroded him emotionally. He could never make sense of something that when it was over had all seemed in vain.

He was so fixated on being nice to the terrier that he didn't recognize the approach of the woman who now stood before him, casting half a shadow over him. As he looked up he recognized the beloved features of his mom's face.

A smile—comrades who knew him in the trenches would say the first smile they ever saw on his face—livened his sullen features until he beamed with happiness. While his heart danced with a joyous rhythm, tears welled in his eyes.

In that instant a lifetime of loneliness was shed.

Love had conquered evil.

26

The French poilus sat side by side with the German infantrymen as they surveyed the fields of Verdun.

"Look at how green, how pleasant the rolling landscape appeals to one's eyes," a former German artilleryman said with admiration in his voice. During the year-long murder that surrounded one of France's most sacred sites, his cannon piece alone must have fired over sixty thousand shells toward the French lines. A small number when one considers that well over two and a half million shells were emitted from the giant Krupp cannons of the Imperial German Army during the year-long battle.

Heaven's Verdun was the way nature looked before the generals decided to decapitate the top layers of land that gave that part of the French countryside its impeccable breathtaking beauty.

It was the way it looked before the armies of le Francais and der Fatherland dug their trenches and altered the original landscape with their endless ditches and their piles of barbed wire which were so thick even artillery shells could not dislodge or destroy them.

It was the way it was before Verdun had become the world's largest cemetery of unburied bodies which lay for weeks and months in heaps amid quagmires of mud while rats by the thousands feasted on the dead flesh of God's children, ignorant of the nationality they gnawed on at all times of the day and night.

A French soldier passed another bottle of Bordeaux between them while plates of fresh Tomme Brulee and Buche de Touraine were shared among the few dozen ex-combatants.

Jean Beaulieu, whose name coincidentally means "beautiful place," settled his empty wine glass beside him and inhaled deeply while soaking in the visual artistry that they all continued to enjoy between victuals and spirits.

"I grew up in Verdun," he proudly announced so everyone could hear. "Before the war, to just sit, just like we are doing now, though more often than not I was in the company of a lovely mademoiselle. I remember how fresh the air was. As we sit here now as brothers it is the first time since I entered the trenches in autumn 1916 up until I died as spring was approaching the following year that I can enjoy the fresh air that compliments that land."

"My first day in the trenches I only smelled mud," offered one of the German lads. "I was shot within an hour of reaching my position, and I slumped over and fell into a morass of mud. A bullet had blown apart my shoulder bone and shrapnel from incoming shells nicked both my legs. No one could come to my aide during the ensuing bombardment and I laid face first breathing in the dampness of the earth. While the blasts sent geysers of earth upward which then fell back down upon me, I pushed my face farther and farther into the soil as though I could possibly hide myself from my fears. I couldn't tell if it was blood seeping from my wounded legs or the water and mud of the hole which I seemed to be sinking in deeper and deeper. Eventually I was submerged up to my neck. Another large-caliber shell deposited a huge amount of earth on top of me but by then my arms were so laden with mud and water that I couldn't use them to brush my head clean. When I yelled for help it only allowed for growing volumes of watery soil to fall into my mouth. I began to choke and fear overwhelmed my body. I could feel air leaving my lungs only to be replaced by more of the slimy liquid that was sliding down my throat and taking my life. It went dark before I closed my eyes for the last time as another dumping of earth from more bomb blasts completely covered me. I don't know how long it took for me to die, all I can remember is that it was painful and I was alone."

He ended recalling his tale by inhaling a huge gulp of fresh air which gave him great satisfaction.

Jean poured his new friends another glass of Bordeaux. All of those present had experienced a similar demise during the bleeding of the French and German armies in the attrition of Verdun. The whole debacle had been so horrific that even in heaven it would be remembered and talked about and if dwelled upon too long would result in sadness creeping its way into the hearts of the conversationalists.

On this day, however, the day of days as some were calling it, they would not let the sadness win, or even get a foothold, for that matter. They continued to enjoy the pristine atmosphere and the magnificent landscape of heaven's Verdun. The freshness of the land and the air cleansed their souls and minds of any residue of ugliness that their generals had heaped upon them during the war. Here they were united in spirit and spirits. They were brothers and friends. They had been waiting for the moment for over a century.

It felt so nice to be alive.

27

In another section of heaven known as the Valley of the Lilies, that same crisp, fresh air hit against the faces of a trio of young horsemen engaged in a spirited half-mile sprint.

Prior to the war, Albert Wegler resided on a small farm in Bavaria. He had grown up caring for and riding the horses that were a part of his family's farm.

Jason Kittle was raised in the wide open spaces of Oklahoma and was helping his father and grandfather break wild mustangs before he was even a teenager.

Ahmet Oztran had ridden horses all of his short life until he was killed as an infantryman in the slime and disease that was part of the Battle of Gallipoli.

As they thundered neck and neck and neck toward the young sapling that they had designated as the finish marker of their race, the smiles that highlighted their joy at being reunited with a passion of their childhood illuminated each of their faces. The three of them had only met less than a quarter of an hour ago as they crossed paths as they entered the valley. They had been informed there were wild horses in the valley for the riding. They were kindred spirits who had never met in life, but the second they saw one another in heaven knew they shared the same fervor for riding.

They had patted the first black, shiny-haired stallion that they encountered with a sense of awe. The smoothness of its well-kept mane brought back mutual feelings of how beautiful the animal was, contrasted with the way the war violated such pristine gifts of nature from God to humans to respect and enjoy.

"The last horse I saw was struggling to pull a wagon of shells to the gunners firing down on the Australians," said Ahmet. "I remember the strain on its face. It was forlorn. It looked abused. It looked like it was asking me to help him, and I remember how sad I felt inside watching such a beautiful creature being worn down and wasted being used against its will to assist in the killing of other creatures who were just as doomed."

"He reminds me of Addie, the first horse I ever rode," said Albert. "I knew from the moment I mounted him that he and I were going to be friends." Jason and Ahmet shared an approving grin as Albert related his memories.

"Then you should be the one who gets to ride him," said Jason, with Ahmet nodding in approval. Without hesitation they assisted Albert in mounting his newfound Addie.

"Shortly before I was killed near Catigny I remember seeing a horse collapsing and dying within seconds," Jason respectfully recalled as he patted Addie on the side as Albert shifted his body to comfortably position himself.

Albert looked at Jason and Ahmet in acknowledgement that he was set and ready to ride. He took a deep breath of satisfaction and closed his eyes as he let out a long exhale. His mind brought back the last images of his beloved horses the day he had died alongside them during a long bombardment. The horses weren't his in the legal sense, it was that they were horses, animals he loved more than anything else in the world. In Albert's mind, all horses were his, that's just the way he felt about them. His first weeks at the front were especially upsetting because he had seen so many horses killed in a never-ending variety of horrendous ways.

On the last day of his life a British bombardment had caught a supply column that he was a part of out in the open and the shells rained down upon soldiers and animals with equal ferocity and deadly results. Less than a minute into the attack, hot shrapnel sliced through both of Albert's legs and he laid their disabled and exposed as the slaughter progressed in front of him. Horses by the dozens, harnessed together pulling wagons with hundreds of pounds of supplies were left exposed to the mercy of the British cannons as their human protectors ran in every direction looking for cover in attempts to save themselves. The rate of falling shells was so intense that no one even attempted to rescue Albert, dooming him to suffer the same fate as his beloved horses.

As he painfully and slowly bled out, evil's handiwork made sure his last moments of life were filled with an ugliness that tortured his soul. Horses being hit with artillery shells exploded into hundreds of clumps of detached flesh and hair. A pumping muscle from a front leg landed near where Albert suffered. A head with the bridle still in place landed in front of him and brushed his arm as it skimmed by like a rock flicked across a calm river. Blood that he knew wasn't from the deep cuts in his legs splattered his face and eyes. While he wiped his eyes clear his senses focused on the high-pitched shrills of the horses whinnying in lost agony. The sharpness of their unabated cries seemed to be louder than the blasts of the artillery shells which covered up any of the sounds being offered up by the soldiers.

Albert could feel his body dying and as he lost the power to wipe away the feces of war from his face and eyes he began to question the insanity of the scene. He didn't think he was loud in his exhortations but survivors of the attack would always recall the private shouting above the dim of battle, "Save the horses! They are beautiful! Save them!"

He wiped the moisture away from his eyes as the nightmarish memory faded and the present brought him back to the glory that was in front of him. Ahmet and Jason nodded at him as if to acknowledge that they recognized that he was momentarily preoccupied with thoughts from the war.

"Let's race," Jason said.

They thundered ahead side by side for the entirety of the race. They exuded youth, camaraderie, and exuberance for life. As they stretched toward the finish line, they were enthralled with the new memories they were making as friends who shared a love of horses and riding. Jason won out by less than a nose on the orange-red-haired mustang he rode with such fury. He had foregone a saddle, comfortable enough on an old, worn-out blanket that was brought to him before they began their race by his mom. It was the one she had hand-stitched for him and presented to him on his thirteenth birthday, along with his first horse, a young orange-red-haired wild mustang his father had spent months trying to corral for him.

Ahmet came in third and was the first to spout out the challenge for another race. Jason smiled and nodded in the affirmative. Albert was already galloping back to where they had started their contest, the juices of excitement shooting through his veins.

It was as beautiful and peaceful a moment as one could find in the Valley of the Lilies.

28

God strolled across the landscape with a smile emblazoned upon his face that would make any child feel the appreciative warmth of approval being bestowed upon him by a loving parent. He was enjoying the moments of the Grand Reunion as much as anyone else. There was great satisfaction upon meeting personally with those of the flock who had maintained their undying belief in the goodness of humans, made in God's image. War had placed so many individuals in the unfair situation of having to declare their selfishness for their own lives at the expense of others who would have to die or even be killed by said individual in order to go on living their own earthly existence.

However, throughout the war, in all armies, numerous soldiers put their own lives in peril in order to save the lives of comrades, sometimes their lifelong friends, more often than not people who they did not know. The majority of them lost their lives in the process of emulating the preaching of the scriptures which said, "There is no greater love than laying down one's life for another."

Allan Rutherford spent day after day during the Battle of the Argonne Forest leaving the safety of his position in order to retrieve wounded soldiers, both American and German, from the battlefield. He was a medic who eventually gathered in over a hundred of God's flock amid the slaughter in the once scenic woods. As shells exploded and shards of shrapnel mixed with splinters from the branched canopy that was shredded by the artillery of Yankee and German industrial might and death rained down upon the wounded, Allan would protect them with his body. Wounds scarred his neck and the back of his hands from the countless times he used himself as a shield to ward off the cascade of debris that fell like droplets of rain in the heat of battle.

The German lad was alive with wounds to his legs that were not life-threatening but were paralyzing enough to prevent him from getting to his own feet and trying to save himself. Allan hovered over him speaking to him with his limited high school German skills being tested for the first time in his life. His words were sufficient enough to calm him down while Allan began to bandage his legs. As the shelling increased in tenacity, Allan threw himself on top of the young soldier to protect him. The sliver of steel which sliced through Allan's neck killed him instantly.

His buddies found his dead body hunched over the young soldier of the Kaiser's army. They became enraged at the fact that he died while saving one of the enemy. They swore and yelled at the frightened German to stand up but all he could do was cry out in his native tongue that he was wounded and . . . it didn't matter because they shot him anyway. The two Americans carried Allan's deceased body back to their command post to prepare him for a proper burial while they left the German who they murdered to rot in the early autumn air.

Joachim Pressler and Vincenzo Cappeletti worked side by for six days during the Battle of Caporetto. Up until those days in October 1917, the young German and the older Italian had never known one another nor would they ever have thought as they grew to like one another in their shared time that they would die together. On opposing sides in the midst of another battle which would see hundreds of thousands killed and maimed from both armies as well as those of the Austrian army, Joachim and Vincenzo were caught up in the circumstances of war that are hard to explain other than they just happened to happen the way they happened.

Joachim was a rifleman while Vincenzo was a doctor. Joachim had been wounded when a bullet grazed the top of his kneecap during the early stages of an attack by Italian troops. Though the wound was not debilitating, it was Joachim's chance to get out of the war albeit by becoming a prisoner. He fell to the ground clutching his leg while other comrades were shot dead around him or began their flight to the rear in the face of an Italian onslaught. Advancing soldiers bypassed him in pursuit of other German soldiers but a few of the secondary troops in the attack raised him to his feet and assisted him toward the Italian medical tents which had been set up close to the frontlines. Once there, Joachim was tenderly cared for by the caring hands of a gentle middle-aged doctor from Orvieto, a classic Italian village about an hour's train ride from Rome.

Vincenzo Cappeletti was a surgeon who had already lost two sons in the war. His wife lost control of her mental faculties after being notified of the death of their second son and spent time in an institution where she died from malnutrition and sickness. The reality was she was so broken by the death of her children that she withdrew from life and just let death slowly take a piece of her day after day until there was no life left for her to live. It was a war statistic that no one kept track of in any of the belligerent nations, but it happened every day to untold numbers of mothers and fathers who couldn't grasp the finality of their children's lives. After the death of his beloved Maria Angela, to whom he had been married for twenty-seven years, Vincenzo decided that he would join the military as a doctor in order to try and save as many lives as possible of children of other parents. He closed his private practice and joined the Italian military.

Dr. Cappeletti and Private Pressler exchanged simple smiles the first time they met. Even though Joachim had tried to tell the Italian soldiers who brought him to the medical tent that his wound was minor and that he could stand, they showed no response that would intimate that they understood him. They took his gun and helmet away and forced him to lie down on a stretcher. A faded wool blanket was thrown over top of him and he was left lying on the ground among dozens of other wounded soldiers, both German and Italian.

Before Vincenzo could say anything to him, Joachim surprised the doctor by telling him in fluent Italian that he was only suffering from a slight wound to the knee, and that it no longer even hurt.

"Where did you learn your Italian?" the doctor asked in a pleasing tone as he pulled the blanket away in order to examine Joachim's knee. A patch of Joachim's uniform was torn away exposing the wound. The bullet had removed a small chunk of skin near the top of his knee but not deep enough to cause any interior damage to the leg. In fact, the bleeding had already stopped and was beginning to dry. Dr. Cappeletti used a liquid antiseptic to wash the wound clean and placed a saintly white bandage on top of the wound.

"My parents never wanted language to be a barrier to me when it came to meeting people," Joachim said with pride. "They began teaching me Italian since I could read and write German, and I'm pretty good at speaking English as well."

Vincenzo finished taping the bandage in place while he listened to the pleasant voice that reminded him of his sons. Neither one in particular, for every young soldier he encountered reminded him of his sons.

"You know, before the war, I wanted to be a doctor," said Joachim, "but in the German army they don't care what you want to be. We're expected to fight and die for God and country and the Kaiser." His voice dropped off in disappointment.

Vincenzo offered his hand to Joachim in order to help him rise from the stretcher. As they met face to face, Joachim looked into the doctor's eyes and with a renewed energy in his voice proudly stated, "I refuse to kill another human. I've been in the front lines for over six months now and I know I haven't killed anyone. I shoot my rifle but I make sure that I'm not aiming at anyone."

A sense of warmness reverberated throughout Vincenzo's body. It was a good, pleasant feeling. He placed a hand on Joachim's shoulder. "I haven't turned away anyone I've found in need since I've come to the front. I have fixed up Italians, Germans, and Austrians. They are all people in need of help." He sighed as though suddenly fatigued. "Since my sons and my wife have died, I no longer see anyone as a nationality."

Joachim seemed to understand all of the feelings the good doctor was emoting. Over the next quarter of an hour, they stood together and talked, as old friends might do upon meeting one another at a coffee shop or a deli for a bite to eat. In the end, they decided that Joachim would not be processed as a prisoner of war, but that he would stay at the front line and work alongside Vincenzo as his new medical orderly. Over the next six days the two of them aided over 250 wounded soldiers from both armies.

The intensity of the battle was so savage that fighting sometimes raged right outside of the tents where they administered life-saving procedures. Joachim was a fast learner and with the amount of casualties coming in at a steady pace hour after hour there were more wounded than available doctors or nurses. He found himself learning how to be a doctor on the spot, aiding Vincenzo in everything from removing bullets from shattered bodies to performing operations on lacerated livers and chest wounds where on one occasion he watched the last heartbeats of a young Italian soldier no older than himself as life stopped in his hands.

Amidst all of their life-saving work, Joachim and Vincenzo were unaware that the ward of tents they were working in actually changed hands from Italian control to German control four times in the last six days. No one from either side seemed to find the time to inform them of the ever-changing events. All they knew hour after hour after hour is that another wounded person was being brought before them. They hardly ever noticed the nationality of the soldier they were trying to save and would have been surprised to know that sometimes the wounded were brought in to them by Italian soldiers and when the facility had changed hands they were being brought in by German soldiers.

At the end of the sixth day the fighting ended as though a light switch was turned off by the night watchman. It was unannounced and quiet and the silence of shell fire and machine guns caught the attention of Vincenzo and Joachim as they finished the last part of a procedure on a wounded Italian soldier who couldn't have been more than seventeen years of age. They smiled at one another in silent, mutual appreciation of their work and in recognition of the cease-fire which brought the calming sound of silence with it.

That sacred moment of serenity was annihilated by evil within seconds. Bursting into their ward entered a weathered soldier in a mud-encased overcoat, so caked that it made interpreting the wearer's nationality impossible to gauge. Sadly it didn't matter. Without warning or explanation the delusional officer raised his pistol and propelled bullets into Joachim's face, Vincenzo's chest, and a third into the head of the wounded boy whose life had so recently been saved by the now dead duo.

The slight breeze gently touched their faces as God presented himself to them.

"Welcome to my home." His voice was gentle and filled with love.

Allan Rutherford stood side by side with Dr. Vincenzo Cappeletti and Joachim Pressler. They were awestruck by the presence of their Lord, as well as the angels who flanked His sides. With reverence they dropped down on bended knee.

God approached them and with outstretched arms raised over them, blessed them in the name of all that is good within heaven and His Kingdom. Their bodies felt invigorated with the eternal spirit of love and they could feel a metamorphosis of body and soul as it transformed their mortal beings.

As God stepped back, his accompanying duo stepped forward and introduced themselves to the now changed trio.

"I am Michael, the Archangel."

"I am Rachmiel, the Angel of Mercy."

In unison they read from the parchment that they shared holding.

"In adhering to the divine commitment of bestowing mercy and charity upon God's children in times of great adversity, and by your lifelong actions of rejecting and denying the admittance of evil into your soul, the wings, and the status, of angel are hereby granted and bestowed upon each of you."

Their reward had been great. They were the first of a select group to be deemed "Angels of the Grand Reunion."

God flashed them a parting smile as he continued on his way to meet and greet the others of the Grand Reunion.

29

The alluring aroma of fresh-baked cinnamon croissants and warm sweet apple muffins mingled together throughout the spacious Saint Elizabeth Bakery. Raspberry and blueberry jam-filled donuts occupied display cases by the hundreds of dozens. A multitude of coffee flavors percolated their enticing tastes through the atmosphere. Fresh milk straight from the cow, or goat, if that was your fancy, was in endless availability. While one could eat till his heart, and stomach, was content, the deadly sin of gluttony was nowhere to be found in the true land of endless milk and honey.

Families long estranged due to wartime deaths recalled old memories of homemade breakfasts or precious baked goods that had exited their lives as their loved ones went off to be part of the great destruction of their generation. Much like their dining room or kitchen tables that had been the focal point of their daily family gatherings prior to their being killed and not returning home, those who had been kept apart all those years were now together again in another of the great gathering halls that dotted heaven's endless landscape.

One of the great stories among many taking place within the confines of Saint Elizabeth Bakery was the coming together of talent sharing the kitchen where all of the fine delectable delights were being created.

Jean Tessier was a poilu during the war; at least that's what it said on the official roster of the unit of which he was a member. Though all French enlisted men were seen as soldiers, Jean's daily responsibility was cooking meals for hundreds of hungry soldiers who were stuck in the trenches trying to survive another day of boredom, monotony, dankness, putrid odors of decaying bodies, rain, mud, and the ever-present sudden death due to artillery shells falling down upon them. There wasn't much to cooking for hundreds at a time, all you did was drop the multitude of ingredients you could find into a rather large vat filled with water, boil it to make sure it was hot, and get it to the troops while there was still some degree of warmth to it so they could pretend that they had experienced a hot meal at least once every few days.

Joseph Mykowski had withstood his fair share of abuse from fellow doughboys when he tried to pass off to them on a daily basis the dark liquid he called coffee. At least he took some comfort in being able to say it was a hot liquid that the boys could feel course through their body and provide some momentary relief to their cold bones on an early fall morning in the trenches somewhere in France.

The British lad, Alan Applecake, had always figured with a name like that that he was born to be a baker and chef. He walked among the others offering up to them a taste of his childhood favorite, Bakewell Pudding. The warm, fresh-baked almond flavor danced across their taste buds and brought expressions of pleasure and satisfaction to the face of everyone.

"The children especially are going to be delighted with your exquisite treats," said his brother in baking, Fahim Atan. "I never tasted something like that myself growing up in Istanbul." Alan smiled at the words of praise and watched as Fahim took another helping of Bakewell Pudding with him on his way back over to his work area.

With a gentleness that evoked the care of a master artist, Fahim slowly opened the oven door and retrieved his own masterpiece. The intoxicating aroma of warm cinnamon wafted about mixing with the flavor of sweet honey that filtered through the kitchen. The slightly golden-brown flaky top perfectly complimented the variety of walnuts, pistachios, and hazelnuts that Fahim liked to include in what he called his own "three-flavored baklava."

Jean's senses were enticing him to go take a taste of Fahim's fanciful pastry, but he was juggling a few of his own divine creations as well. The baklava would have to wait until later. Jean was busy finishing the presentation of his Parisian Macarons. Variety was Jean's specialty. The light but crunchy shells of each treat laid out in separate rows on a silver platter highlighted tastes including the simple, comforting sensation of vanilla, sweet dark chocolate with bits of cocoa mixed in for a little extra zest, and Jean's favorite, the tart taste of raspberry mixed with the divine flavor of lychee.

After placing a number of trays of macarons in the glass case at the counter, Jean turned his attention to the Bichon Au Citron. Children by the scores were staring with glee in their eyes at the partially caramelized puff pasties that filled sheet after cooking sheet. Jean could see it in their faces that they were already imagining the exquisite taste of the refreshing lemon Bavarian cream that would soon be squirting to all sides of their mouth with that initial bite in which each of them would soon partake.

Jean's finale was the Coussin de Lyon. He couldn't resist popping two in his mouth at the same time, allowing the explosion of flavors to morph with one another. The marzipan and the chocolate ganache, dare one say, was a heavenly mixture that satiated the palate of anyone who shared Jean's talents for crafting a taste no one could deny or turn away from.

Catching a glimpse of joy on Jean's face made Joseph Mykowski emote a look of self satisfaction as well. He had been baking shortly after his arrival earlier in the day and had already not only prepared but helped serve nearly fifty of his good old fashioned American-made, home-style, homemade version of his mom's Addison, Wisconsin, apple pie. The entire time he was stationed in France he hadn't even had an apple and being involuntarily denied the pleasure of his favorite taste of home played havoc with his emotions especially in the fall during harvest season, when he knew that back home everyone would be picking fresh bushels of sweet delights. Thanksgiving at the front was especially hard where for the first and only time in his life he had been denied apple pie on his favorite holiday.

Joe's secret to a pie that served up a flavor with more zest and tang to it than most any other apple pies the world over was having the patience to pare and include an equal amount of sweet, tart Honeycrisp apples with firm yellow-green Crispin apples as well as Cripps Pink apples which when baked together with the right amount of cinnamon as well as an extra dash for some kick would send taste buds into a tizzy of tasteful sensations. Topped with a scoop of freshly whipped French vanilla ice cream, the dessert was the most eagerly sought after treat in Saint Elizabeth's Bakery. The rumor going around was that God wanted to have two slices of Joe Mykowski's Wisconsin Apple Pie but didn't want to give the impression that he had fallen victim to gluttony so when he stopped in the bakery later in the day he settled for just the one piece, though he desperately wanted to enjoy a second tasting. Some of the angels were even saying it was one of the few times they had ever seen God sad.

The German baker Rudi Steinwehr had heard the story making the rounds about God's reaction to his friend's apple pie. Like everyone else who was baking that morning, Rudi believed God reacted the way he did because he only tried one dessert during his time visiting the bakery. Surely, Rudi thought, if God had tried his delectable triangle-shaped hamantash pocket pastry filled with a choice of palate pleasing poppy seed, exquisite savory cherry, or his sweet nectarine and apricot combo, God would have requested a dozen to take with him. Rudi took solace knowing that since they would be hanging around heaven for a long time, God would eventually return to try one of his pastry Renoirs and he was sure that after that first taste, God would never think about eating Wisconsin Apple Pie again.

30

The young lawyer with the round glasses looked as young as he did the day he drowned. The majority of empty souls who had been spiritually killed by the war ended their lives with a quick shot from a pistol or a rifle, more times than not with the same or similar style weapon they had used throughout the Great War.

Charles Whittlesey opted for the moment that would allow him to disappear from society without the messy cleanup that no one ever talks about after a person has carried out their act of final expression. Suicide was never painless, for the victim or those they left behind who had to deal with the reality that their loved one had departed them in such an unexpected and self-induced violent way. A suicide note that was left with the intention of explaining why the decision was made to carry out the act usually only led to more questions being asked by the survivors.

The former captain of the Lost Battalion of the United States 77th Division tried to understand as much of his wartime experiences as he could before being overwhelmed by his feelings of despair and disillusion.

Like many, he became withdrawn. His days of peace in the postwar world were consumed by the internal conflict that raged between his conscience and mental ability to comprehend his experiences in the Argonne Forest. The image of his friend being shredded into so many pieces by a direct hit from an artillery shell, one dropped upon him by his own American gunners, never exited his thoughts.

Seeing so many young men who had put their faith in him as their leader killed by his incompetence, or so he thought and, worse, believed, never allowed him a moment's respite despite an armistice just a few weeks after his experience. His short post-war existence was nothing more than long days of agony. Despite being awarded the Congressional Medal of Honor for his actions which saved 194 men of his battalion, Charles was never comfortable with the accolades. When compelled to speak in public about his wartime experiences, he always talked about the bravery of the men under his command. Never did he highlight his own bravery.

The conclusion of any speaking engagement about the battalion's exploits was followed by endless hours of a self-imposed mental beating. The questions never left the forefront of his thinking. He would sit alone in a room staring endlessly into the past reflecting and questioning himself.

"Would they all be alive today if I hadn't sent the wrong coordinates to the artillery gunners?"

"How many men were killed because I didn't do enough to save them?"

"How do you move on with your life when all those boys were killed because of you?"

His last thoughts before he jumped off the SS *Toloa*, a steamship bound for Cuba, into the depths of the ocean were with his men, apologizing to them for their deaths right up until the water sucked the last breath out of his body and he drowned alone, never to be found by those who desperately searched for him once they realized what events had unfolded.

Now, he stood there in heaven along a path in the midst of a lovely forest area which was more peaceful than anything he had experienced while living on Earth. The rich green pines gave off a comforting scent that made him feel relieved of any self guilt. His lungs sucked in the freshness of the air and he could sense his body being alive. He gently wiped clean the round lens of his eyewear and his attention was attracted to the gentle cooing of a small pigeon that fluttered its way toward him. Securing his glasses around his earlobes, he stared at the pigeon which was strutting at his feet while constantly craning its head upward as if asking Charles for positive recognition.

Whittlesey broke into a grin of satisfaction as he reached down to pet the head of the small animal.

"I know who you are, Cher Ami," he whispered softly as he calmly stroked her feathers. He was greeted with a constant cooing of satisfaction. "Nice to see you with both of your legs." While carrying a message written by Whittlesey to the artillery gunners to stop the bombardment of their own men, the carrier pigeon Cher Ami had one of its feet shot off by German soldiers who were trying to stop the pigeon from carrying out its mission. The French, upon hearing of the pigeon's bravery, awarded Cher Ami the Croix de guerre.

From around a turn down the road Whittlesey could begin to hear the sound of singing. Securing Cher Ami in his arms like carrying a football, Charles could see coming into view a large group of people. They were in no particular order but looked more like picnickers on a Sunday outing. Smiles on their faces were evidence of the glee and joy they were experiencing. Children scampered around or skipped about to the melody of their tune, "In the Good Old Summertime." The grown-ups continued to sing while some exchanged kisses or hugs with one another as they got closer to where Whittlesey was standing. Out of uniform they looked different than he remembered them, but when they stopped in front of him and began a three-cheers chant for him he began to recognize the young men of his battalion.

There was Abraham Krotoschinsky, the young private he helped calm down in the face of enemy fire and who survived the ordeal of the Argonne.

Next to him was Benjamin Gaedeke, his dear friend who Charles last saw being blown to pieces by one of the misguided rounds from his own American artillery.

Stepping through the crowd was George McMurtry. Though severely wounded during the battle, he had continued to be a foundation of leadership for Whittlesey as well as the rest of the battalion until they were found and relieved by other American troops. He hugged Charles so hard that Cher Ami almost got squished. Tears began to flow down Whittlesey's cheeks in unabashed sentimentality.

One by one they made their way forward to shake hands with their caring commander.

Homer Rayson and John Ruppe were scouts who had been killed in action.

Patrick Maney, Frederick Wilber, Glenn Weaver, reliable privates who had been wounded.

James Slingerland, Isadore Ostrovsky, Hugo Untereiner, some of the living who had shared the horrors and lived to carry the nightmares with them the rest of their lives, shook Whittlesey's hand with gusto.

The acts of gratitude and love continued until all 554 members of the battalion had reintroduced themselves to their former major.

Benjamin Gaedake stepped forward once again, his wife at his side.

"We got together earlier today, Major, near the entrance where St. Peter was greeting everyone. We wanted to come to you as one group, but we also wanted our families to come with us so they could meet you as well. We—"

"I'm sorry so many of you died because of me—"

His reaction was cut off by a chorus of nos, an instantaneous response that harkened forth from everyone in the battalion. The response was so emotional that it caught Whittlesey by surprise and he ceased his apology in midsentence. He was in awe of the loyalty his men were showing on his behalf.

Gaedeke began again after the last no finally dissipated into heaven's atmosphere. "You gave of yourself for our benefit every time you made a decision and with every order you gave us to follow, sir. The friendly fire incident was not your fault. It was just a reality of the ugliness of war. Your anguish on our behalf is understood more than you realize, but it is unwarranted, and we do not accept it. No commander had more affection for his troops than you did, sir." With a fury they let loose a three-cheers chant for their former major.

Gaedeke smiled with honor while Whittlesey choked back more tears, this time ones of pride. He cleared his throat to make himself heard by everyone. "I am overwhelmed at seeing all of you again," he began, gaining more strength in his delivery as he continued. "All I ever wanted was to make sure that you would be able to go home and see your families again, and enjoy your lives with them."

Now it was their turn to weep and their emotions openly flowed forward. He held his composure as he finished, "It is so comforting that we are no longer lost, rather that we are together, happy and in the home of our Lord."

31

Altan Basak had barely made it through the gates of heaven when it all began to appear before his very eyes.

He could see.

Early in the Gallipoli campaign a British Mills bomb had sent fragments of the grenade through his eyelids and pierced his iris and retina. The pain that seared through his body let him know that he wasn't dead, but he knew he had been blinded even as his legs buckled and he slumped to the surface of the battlefield.

He could feel strong hands holding his head in place while gentle hands dabbed his face clean of the body fluids which had obscured his skin. His brain was telling him he was trying to open his eyelids so he could recognize what was happening to him but only muted darkness greeted his efforts. In his mind he pictured his wife of one year, Erendiz, and his newborn daughter of only a few weeks, Pinar.

Now it was almost too much to take in at one time. While many were speaking in loud tones in order to combat the natural rise in volume which gradually occurs when thousands and thousands of people are gathered in the vicinity, Altan was more focused on what everyone looked like instead of what they were saying. Trying to take in all the vibrant visual offerings that presented themselves to him was a bit overwhelming after a lifetime of somber darkness, despair, and feeling sorry for one's self. It was difficult to explain the sensations as his eyes experienced the excitement of seeing such things that might usually be perceived as mundane to one who had never lost their sense of sight.

The subtle differences in shades of green between the leaves that gently dangled from the trees which lined the park area around him brought him pleasure. The smiles of so many people in the first throes of reuniting with a long-lost loved one made him think of the sparkling reaction one witnesses when a ray of sun strikes a piece of delicate crystal. The kaleidoscope of hues worn by the crowds made it difficult to focus on any one particular shade or individual until that little gut feeling one experiences when they know something is happening that they can't explain began to envelope his conscience.

Out of the masses emerged an angel . . . *his* angel.

She was wearing a white wedding dress of the brightest, most pure white satin and lace that dulled the tone of every other color Altan had previously viewed. Through her partially open veil he could see Erendiz flashing a soft, enticing smile that reminded him of the day they exchanged their vows. Their love that night had brought more beauty into their lives with the arrival of Pinar nine months later. He was so entranced by the sheer elegance and allure of his wife that he remained speechless until she stood face to face with him. They enjoyed a soft moment of passion as their arms enjoined their bodies and their lips met together.

As they released from their mutual embrace, Erendiz spoke first.

"Since it is like starting over again up here, I thought you would like to see me like you did on the first day of our life as husband and wife."

It took Altan a moment to gather his thoughts.

"All those years after I was blinded, you gave me unconditional love. I only felt sorry for myself. When I finally accepted that I wouldn't see again I emptied my mind of all previous images of you, except of you on our wedding day. Each time I heard your voice when you spoke to me and I didn't respond to you, I was thinking of you as you are now before me."

Altan bowed his head in shame.

"I was so unfair to you. I'm so sorry."

She lifted his chin with her fingertips in the most tenderly way.

"I vowed to love you," Erendiz said, then leaned forward to kiss him again.

Their reunion was just getting started.

Nine months later Pinar would have a new sister.

32

Five-year-old James Stanton stood hand in hand with his mom, Madison. The sun warmed them. They waited in great anticipation. They had been told by a couple of the Benedictine monks they encountered when they first entered heaven that those who had been victims of the Zeppelin bombing of London in May 1915 could most likely find family members in this region, known as The Cove of Divine Protection. They were among the twenty-eight killed that night in a new form of terror to be experienced by civilians who in the darkness of night were quickly educated to the modern warfare reality that the frontlines were everywhere, shattering the myth of home front safety.

Madison was killed when the second-floor bedroom in which James was sleeping in collapsed on top of her while she sat in the parlor writing a letter to her husband, Douglas, who was with the British army at the moment engaged in the Second Battle of Ypres. James miraculously survived the destruction of his bedroom but was killed in the ensuing fire. Rescue workers found the boy lying next to his mom whose partially hidden body jutted out from under a pile of charred debris. They deduced that the young lad had tried to pull his already dead mother free from the wreckage when he was overcome by smoke inhalation. Most of his body was burned by the ensuing flames.

Douglas survived the Second Battle of Ypres as well as the war itself but spent the rest of his days unable to comprehend why he was allowed to live through so many murderous battles while his family was snatched from him while in the alleged safety of the home he had provided for them. He knew it wasn't his fault, but the inability to comprehend the illogic behind the event haunted him every day for the next fifty-two years of his life.

He caught site of Madison and James as he strode down the dirt road toward the cove. He was accompanied by a man in his early forties who sported a close-cropped haircut, a thick, tight mustache, and a short goatee. Not even the angels who were fluttering about could mistake this man for being anything other than a military personality during his days on earth.

As they got closer, Douglas excused himself from his friend's company and sprinted the last score of yards toward his family. The three of them hugged with such passion and ferocity that they stumbled about amidst their own laughter at how silly they must have looked as their emotions overcame their sense of balance.

After righting themselves, Douglas kissed Madison one more time and then turned to introduce his new friend, who had made his way up to the trio while they were celebrating.

"Honey," Douglas said with the utmost courtesy, "may I present to you Peter Strasser."

Madison reached her hand out to grasp Peter's. James stepped forward and did the same. Peter responded to each in kind.

There followed a moment of awkward silence.

Douglas cleared his throat, held James by the hand, and threw his other arm around Madison.

"Peter led the Zeppelins which bombed London and other places in England. He was killed in the last raid of the war in August 1918."

Peter bowed his head in shame. On the walk over to meet his family, Douglas had explained to Peter what happened to his family during the London raid. Douglas had met Peter while Peter had been seeking out families who had been killed during the raids that he led in order to apologize to them and seek their forgiveness. Needless to say it had been quite an emotional morning so far for the former Zeppelin commander.

Madison stepped forward and hugged Peter. "Have you met your family up here yet?" she asked. "We're okay here," she went on, not waiting for Peter to reply. "Go meet your family first. We have all the time in heaven to enjoy your friendship."

Peter was touched by her kind response. Douglas smiled and chuckled. "I told you she would say that. It's the kind of person she is. It's why I love her so much."

Peter turned to leave and then did an about face. "Me and my family look forward to dining with all of you in the coming weeks. It will be our pleasure."

33

They climbed into their old planes once again with great excitement and enthusiasm coursing through their veins. It was like old times, the glory of their youth all over again. The engine coughed and then caught. The red wings of the Fokker triplane glimmered as the sun bounced off the fresh coat of paint. The wooden propeller of the Sopwith Camel spun into motion. Sans military armaments and any military or national insignia, the planes were the originals flown by the energized pilots. Their paths had crossed once before in one of those extraordinary events of the war that was fought miles above the trenches. Like many of the events which occurred in and above the clouds, they could only be verified by the individuals who experienced them.

In the summer of 1918, the Canadian flier Roy Benson and the German flier Rudi Brauch had met high in the skies over the western front. Upon entering heaven earlier in the day, they sought each other out until they successfully found one another then spent hours reminiscing about their shared wartime experience. Both were out on reconnaissance patrols that fine morning during the waning weeks of the war.

"I was so high in the sky that I felt like I was touching heaven," Roy had told him as they recalled to each other everything that happened that day.

"I always felt that God's hand was resting on my shoulder," Rudi jibed.

"I remember I had the sun behind me," said Roy, "and when I saw you below me I figured you were going to be an easy kill. Once I made my dive on you and got you in my gun sights I knew you were mine for the taking . . . but my guns jammed."

Rudi chuckled at the tale told by his former adversary. "Once you flew by me I realized I had a perfect opportunity to end your flying days. When I pulled the trigger of my guns nothing happened. It took me a few seconds to realize I was out of ammunition."

"So perhaps God was watching over both of us that day," Roy injected.

Rudi stopped laughing and a serious look came over his face. "I never thought of that," he said. "I remember being angry when I got back to my base that day, just being angry that my guns didn't work. I never thought of it being the other way around that something happened to spare my life that day."

"What did you do after the war?" Roy asked.

"I was a carpenter. I helped build houses. I enjoyed the physical labor. I found it rewarding to construct things instead of destroying things."

"I actually did the same thing," Roy said while laughing at Rudi's answer. "I must have helped pound nails into over ten thousand roofs in my post-war days. There was great satisfaction in knowing I helped provide some comfort for a family."

"The feeling of the air rushing against my face never left my senses," Rudi said. "I didn't have a chance to fly after the war for a number of reasons. I always said to myself if I get to heaven then I will fly to my heart's content, so here I am."

"I am glad we got to meet, Rudi," Roy said.

So went the conversation before the two of them, enemies in the war tied together by unusual circumstances, climbed into their beloved planes and took off to enjoy the thrill of flying once again.

34

A short distance away from where Rudi and Roy had taken off, in one of the hangars that stored the refurnished airplanes from the Great War, perfect in every aspect as the originals except void of any weaponry and national or military insignia, another reunion, with a more familial touch to it, was taking place.

Perhaps of all the father and son reunions which were taking place that first day, this one would be ranked as one of the most emotional. The Old Rough Rider from the Spanish-American War in 1898 had been a huge supporter of American intervention in the Great War from its earliest days. Through the years of neutrality he had publicly attacked President Woodrow Wilson with many unkind words to the point of questioning his intestinal fortitude and some say even his patriotism.

Theodore Roosevelt, he of the Big Stick Policy, The Great White Fleet, and a never-ending public commentary championing United States industrial and military power to help establish itself as the new empire in the world, had been one of the most enthusiastic Americans the day Congress finally declared war on the German Empire. The spirit of jingoism not to mention the spirit of pursuing the big adventure in life had been well instilled into his children from the time they could walk and talk.

He beamed with pride when his youngest son, Quentin, became a flier as part of the 95th Aero Squadron and was stationed along the front lines in France. The thought of something negative happening to his American eagle never crossed the old soldier's mind. His world was shattered when word reached him in the security of his home at Sagamore that while flying a mission near Chamery, Quentin was shot down and killed in July 1918. Six months later on January 6, 1919, Teddy himself died.

Nothing in his life had been able to tame the overbearing personality of the great TR, except the death of Quentin, his dear, beloved youngest son. His death sucked the life out of Teddy. In the quiet and emptiness of his large home, Teddy spent long hours brooding over Quentin's death. Alone, the tears flowed for long periods of time. Through hours of quiet self-evaluation, he questioned his gusto and zeal for the war, and worse, the eagerness he had shown in encouraging and supporting Quentin's decision to join up and fight the Hun. Soon he began to blame himself for Quentin's death. It was at that point that he began to understand what all parents who lost sons in the war must be going through. No one else could understand the constant feelings of despair and loneliness. For a great doer of so many accomplishments, such as he was throughout the course of his life, at that moment Roosevelt realized he was powerless. God had humbled him.

Thoughts of Quentin occupied his mind up until the final hours of his life. His last hope and prayer was that God would allow him to be reunited with his son in heaven.

He entered heaven a changed man.

God, not Saint Peter, met him outside the pearly gates. Teddy's first action was to bow down before Him and once again ask for absolution, and the chance to see Quentin at least one more time. God's mercy and justice was placed upon him and along with everyone else that day, he had been granted acceptance into the Kingdom of the Lord.

He stood now in the hangar, alone, next to the Nieuport plane that was Quentin's during the war. He reached in and touched the seat where Quentin sat when he was behind the controls.

"I'll take you for a ride if you want, Father," said Quentin.

Teddy was surprised. He had not heard him coming. As he turned around to face his son, Quentin could already see the emotional overflow dampening his dad's cheeks.

"It is okay, Father," was all Quentin could get out before he found himself being bear hugged by the emotional two-time ex-president and former big game hunter. Teddy was squeezing so hard that Quentin had to ask him to stop in order for him to catch his breath.

"I love you, my son. I am so sorry what happened to you. It was my fault. Please forgive me, I'm so sorry." His words soon became garbled due to the sobbing that overtook his ability to speak clearly.

Quentin could only smile and hug him back, his attempts to console his father by patting him on the back of his head only bringing more emotions out of the old war horse.

It was such a touching scene that even God, watching from the entranceway to the hangar, shed tears.

35

In a quiet grove of elm trees a short distance away, twenty-two-year-old Sidney Howe, sitting with his back against one of the providers of cooling shade, his arms resting on his knees of his drawn up legs, was lost in quiet reflection as he looked at his hands. With slow deliberation his eyes traced each line that crisscrossed his palms. He curled each finger individually and then as a unit producing a tight fist. As he allowed them to open again he marveled at the simplicity of their flexibility. He snapped his fingers, almost as if testing them to see if they really worked, though more likely he did it to convince himself that they were really there.

The young Canadian from Cole Harbour, Nova Scotia, Canada, had been part of the 25th Battalion Nova Scotia Rifles of the Canadian Expeditionary Force fighting as part of the Hundred Days' Offensive between August 26 and August 30, 1918. While Sidney had been among those to celebrate the capture of the towns of Monchy-le-Preux and Wancourt and had come through the battle unscathed, he became a casualty by inadvertently setting off a booby trap set by retreating German soldiers.

The insidiousness of a booby trap lay in the creativity put into making something which appeared to be harmless extremely hazardous to the recipient of the unexpected detonation. Sidney was searching for something to eat in one of the uninhabited houses of Wancourt and went to retrieve what he believed was a canister of cookies or crackers from the top shelf of the pantry. With both hands wrapped around the heavy cream-colored ceramic container, arms stretched overhead as he stood on his tip toes to reach the top shelf, he set off the hand grenade which had been delicately wedged between the canister and the back wall. The explosion detached fingers from the palms of both hands while bone shards mixed with hard ceramic pieces from the canister smacked into Sidney's chin and crown of his rounded helmet. Once the force of the blast subsided, Sidney was lying on his back on the floor of the kitchen dazed and momentarily disoriented.

Then the pain attacked him. It shot from his mangled hands up his arms and alerted his brain to the immense throbbing that pulsated from what was left of what used to be his fingers. They were all gone. His left arm stopped at his wrist, where blood was freely flowing. His right arm ended with a couple inches of palm remaining intact but nothing more.

His pals were aiding him within seconds of the devastating occurrence, a trio of them having witnessed him entering the domicile moments earlier. They quickly stopped the profusion of blood from his now useless appendages but he knew before he blacked out from the oppressive pain that his life was completely altered for the negative.

Sitting in heaven, Sidney was astonished and awed by the wholesomeness of his body, especially his hands.

Tears filled his eyes as he imagined the feel of the wooden shaft of his hockey stick so perfectly snuggled into the padding of his gloves. He imagined how glorious it would be when he met up with his childhood pals here in heaven and they engaged in a game of frozen pond hockey. Sidney pretended snapping off a quick wrist shot toward the goalie. Just the thought of playing the game again was an emotion of pure love.

It was a wonder how many of these lads who had been disengaged from life due to the wounds inflicted upon them by the violence of the Great War found themselves thinking back to the days of their pre-war youth as they realized what it meant to be in heaven. So many emotions swirled around in their minds that it was understandable how one could think of one thing and not another especially, one that others might think more important in the ranking of priorities.

Sidney's childhood remembrances were displaced by the gentle shadow which entered his visionary realities. He looked up to see his lovely wife. She was beyond beautiful. Even in heaven there weren't any words to convey how much splendor and exquisiteness Sidney saw in her appearance.

"Hello, Sidney," she said in the most demure way fitting a young wife of the Victorian era. Her smile melted his memories of childhood pond hockey interests and lit his emotions as they had not been since that day his hands had been detached from his core. The issues and events he had pushed to the recesses of his subconscious all those years after the war until his death on the eve of the next great world cataclysm flooded his thoughts.

When he woke up in the field hospital he didn't need the surgeons to inform him that his hands were gone. The bandaged stubs that greeted his vision as he opened his eyelids two days hence sent him into an emotional tailspin that he never for a solitary moment the rest of life recovered from in any way one could remotely construe as positive. Returning home to Cole Harbour and his expectant wife one month short of their first wedding anniversary, Sidney showed little outward emotion to his life's love. He had already decided without his hands he was as good as a cadaver. The day Sheila delivered their baby princess Antoinette at the local hospital, Sidney stayed at home. He didn't want to experience the humiliation in public of being a new father and not being able to hold his newborn daughter in his hands. Upon coming home Sheila went to place Antoinette, swaddled in her homemade soft pink cotton blanket, in the crook of his arm. She wanted Sidney to enjoy the experience of being a new father but it was a stillborn effort.

In a terse tone that wallowed in self-pity and would be commonplace the rest of his life, Sidney instructed Sheila to take her back. "You don't know what it means to be useless," he said with the authority of a new invalid who had already given up the fight to make anything positive out of his situation.

Sidney died in 1939 from influenza. Sheila was at his side, as was their ravishing Antoinette, now in her early twenties, never having felt the caring touch of her father's hands her entire life.

Sidney looked into Sheila's celestial blue eyes as she stepped closer. It was like seeing her for the first time all over again. He leapt to his feet and embraced her with such fluidity that he didn't notice the softly cooing baby tucked against her bosom that he almost crushed her with the intensity of his hug. The smile on Sheila's face rivaled the one that graced her appearance throughout the day that they had exchanged their vows. Sheila placed a calming hand on Sidney's shoulder and softly guided him back into a sitting position under the shade of the elm. With a tenderness that only a first time mother could emit, Sheila softly placed the newborn Antoinette into the cupped hands of her father.

Sidney's emotions overwhelmed him. Sheila dabbed the tears which were so plentiful they momentarily blurred his vision. Not only was he holding his newborn child for the first time, he was able to experience touching her. With Antoinette secure in the grasp of his right arm, Sidney let the fingers of his left hand fall as soft as a newly crystallized snowflake upon his child's forehead and cheek. With the tip of his index finger he traced the outline of Antoinette's face and then tapped the tip of her nose as though dotting an exclamation point. All those years taken away from them by the war would be theirs to live again.

Sheila sat next to him and kissed away another tear which was quietly making its way down his cheek. Sidney's free hand made its way from Antoinette's face to Sheila's ring hand. Their fingers intertwined like lattice work. It symbolized the unending love they shared with one another and would enjoy throughout their time in God's kingdom.

36

A most poignant reunion was taking place along the shores of Lake Shiloh. The young Canadian, George Price, formerly of the 38th Northwest Infantry Battalion, watched as his family members approached him at a steady pace. Close by, waiting in just as much anticipation for his family, was Joseph Albert Trebuchon, who met his fate as the result of a well-placed sniper's bullet while delivering a message to his superior, carrying out his duty to the last second of his life. A few feet distant from him, the doughboy Henry Gunther waited impatiently for his girlfriend Olga, from his Baltimore neighborhood from which he left but never returned. Sitting on a boulder closest to the waters of the lake, George Edwin Ellison remembered his last day as a member of the 5th Royal Irish Lancers. His charming wife Hannah and their five-year-old son James Cornelius were the last images on his mind before the blood of life seeped out of him and he lapsed into the deep, dark world of death.

Their reunions were moving in the sense that their deaths during the war stung a little more than others in that each of the soldiers mentioned were the last of the respective armies to be killed in the war. They all shared November 11, 1918, as their death day. While millions of others experienced jubilation as the armistice went into effect at the eleventh hour of the eleventh day of the eleventh month in the fourth year of the obscenity that was the bloodletting that introduced the twentieth century, each of these men were denied that final celebration. Their families, upon being notified of the deaths of their loved ones and the circumstances that surrounded their departures

147

from the earth, sent them into differing states of emotional agony that would stay with them the rest of their natural lives.

None could comprehend the illogic behind continuing the killing that last day up until the final minute agreed upon to end the fighting. As was common throughout the war, nothing was to be gained from their loved ones being killed in vain especially on a day they should have been allowed to celebrate as the day they would remember as the first day of the rest of their lives in trying to live a normal existence once again. Never to be justified, over 2,700 died that last day, with another 11,000 more being wounded.

George Ellison showed no pretext of controlling his emotions upon seeing his beloved Hannah, with son James Cornelius in tow, walking toward him as the warm water of the lake gently lapped against the sandy shore. His tears distorted his vision momentarily, but by the time he was wrapping his arms around the two of them, everything about the entire sight taking place was perfect.

George Price was always reserved in life and was so now, at least in outward appearances. Holding hands with family members, feeling the softness of their touch, and the love that was transferred through the simple act of laying a hand into the palm of another hand, or wrapping a hand around one's neck and hugging tight and close, seemed to discount the need to express anything verbally at least for the initial moments.

Henry Gunther just cried as Olga held him close. Later in the day they would take time to plan their wedding just as they had so many years ago, though this time nothing would stop it from taking place.

Joseph Albert Trebuchon celebrated by jumping into Lake Shiloh fully clothed, pulling in a number of family and friends who regardless of being taken for an unexpected swim refused to physically let loose of his arms or legs. As the water overlapped their heads they finally released their grasps but were quick to grab hold again of their beloved Joseph once they broke the surface for a gasp of air. The joy was overwhelming. They could celebrate as carefree as they wanted for nothing negative was going to happen to them, not anymore.

Things like that just didn't happen in heaven.

37

"Good-bye, Mother, I will see you in the next life."

They were the last words of the last letter that Vyacheslav Timinov had written to his mother the day before his unit entered the battle. Like much of the fighting on the Russian front during the war, the battle was not big enough to warrant everlasting fame, but it did contribute significantly to the butcher's bill. Even though Timinov's group outnumbered the German soldiers they were facing that day, they were not adequately supplied to give them a chance to defeat their enemy. Their commanding officers knew before even sending them into combat that a great majority of their peasant soldiers would become casualties. In fact, almost half of the Russian army had no weapon other than bare hands and an emotional desire to fight for the Motherland. Unarmed, Timinov's orders were to follow those with weapons into the battle and when one of them were killed he would retrieve a weapon from the fallen and kill as many Germans as possible until he was killed and the man following him would be able to arm himself.

It was as though Lucifer himself was in command of the Russian armies and couldn't rub his hands together fast enough in glee at the death toll that would be exacted each time the army of the Czar went into battle. Timinov's body was found afterward with so many bullets in it that it resembled a cheese grater. Unceremoniously it was tossed into a mass grave by surviving soldiers who couldn't bury the number of dead quick enough to ward off bodies bloating and millions of flies from finding a free feast.

They sat in heaven at a small wooden table next to a charming creek that soothingly trickled by at a pace which invited one to sit by and relax. Vyacheslav was enjoying a bowl of solyanka, his favorite soup that his mom had made for him so many times as young boy. The cured meat and sausage pieces mixed with a handful of olives, capers, pickles, carrots, and sliced sweet cabbage in a hot broth sprinkled with dill and a light touch of sour cream was as good in heaven as it was when his mother made it for him in their Ukrainian village where they lived before the war took away those comfortable moments of life they had so often enjoyed.

Neither of them said much as they sat across from one another and enjoyed each other's company in relative silence. Neither had been very demonstrative with their emotions in life and their faith in a next world was not something that was idle rhetoric while they lived out their time on earth. Their joy was just as ecstatic as that being experienced by so many others, they just expressed it in a more quiet subdued way.

As Vyacheslav slurped the last spoonful of broth, his mother reached across the table for the empty bowl. She gazed at him the way mothers around the world upon seeing their child after a long absence tend to do with that look on their face which hides a repressed, internal happiness that everyone knows they are experiencing. It was a quiet expression of satisfaction and contentment that everything was good again.

"Would you like another serving?" she asked, knowing ahead of time what his response would be.

"Please, mother," Vyacheslav responded with a smile of contentment. Nothing more needed to be said as they enjoyed the moment and in their own way basked in the wonders of the grand reunion.

38

Twenty-nine-year old Otto Reibeck could feel the blood ever so slowly ooze forth from the shrapnel wound in his thigh. He didn't know what to make of it as the battle raged around him. It hurt. There was a continual throbbing in his leg where the jagged piece of iron had torn into him. It was so hot that tiny wisps of smoke emitted from the metal as well as the wound. His mind was a scramble of thoughts. Was he in shock? Why wasn't he screaming like he had seen other wounded soldiers scream? If he could feel the pain but wasn't screaming, maybe it wasn't that bad of a wound. If so, then why couldn't he move? Maybe it was fear more than the severity of the wound that was keeping him on the ground?

Machine gun bullets kicked up the dirt to his left. Was some French gunner trying to finish him off? Why was he being singled out? He heard a heavy thump coming from behind him, like someone hitting a sandbag with a thick stick. The source of the sound tripped over his prostrate body and fell forward a few feet before landing face down on the ground. Otto could see a round hole tinged with blood in the back of the dead soldier, most likely the exit point of the bullet which had entered his chest.

Otto dragged himself despite his wound until he was side by side with the dead soldier. Lying on his back and staring upward, Otto could see the image of another oncoming German soldier enter his field of vision. Just as quick as he appeared he disappeared from his sight but not before Otto witnessed the side of the soldier's face being shattered from multiple bullets. It was like seeing a mini watermelon explode on hitting the ground after being dropped from a high distance. The body of the dead man lay crumpled directly in front of Otto. Two bullets thumped into it making Otto realize that the deceased was now a source of protection for himself.

Otto felt lightheaded and weak. His mind continued to flutter from thought to thought. Is this what it's like to die? A tinge of pain coursed through his leg to his brain. *I can't be dead yet if I still feel the agony,* he surmised. He opened his eyes to see the sky above him. How useless to be a wounded soldier lying on his back in the middle of a battle. He tuned back in to the war taking place around him. He could hear voices shouting orders, others yelling in fear, other screaming from the pain being inflicted upon them. Sharp sounds like the whistling of bullets ricocheting off stones or maybe the coal scuttle helmets of attacking comrades particularly sharpened his sense of hearing.

The sky darkened as another approaching soldier intruded into his line of vision. He could see the youngster grasp for his throat in an obvious reaction to being shot. Blood spewed forth from the wounded man's mouth and landed on Otto's face. The newest casualty of the war landed on Otto's stomach, his head coming to a rest as though he had planned to cradle himself in Otto's arms. He was gasping for air and Otto could see blood spilling from the man's throat wound as well as his mouth. Otto's uniform acted like a napkin absorbing the man's liquid of life.

Stretching his hands forward, Otto fumbled around in his kit which was still strapped around his waist and did his best to provide comfort to the dying. He tried to staunch the bleeding with a clean undershirt he had produced from his bag. He put pressure on the wound with one hand and with his other was able to open his canteen and gently pour some cool water on the forehead of the dying man. It was impossible to give him a sip of water because of the amount of blood that still effused from his mouth. Otto was unable to ignore the ghastly gurgling sound the man made as he continued to choke to death in his own blood and saliva, but he couldn't do anything to block it out of his senses even amidst the volume of the violence of the war around him. The undershirt Otto was using in vain to staunch the flow of blood had become saturated to the point that it was no longer white but red. The wounded soldier opened and closed his eyelids a few times and then died.

With a dead man cradled in his arms, one alongside of him, and one resting against the top of his head, Otto felt a sense of relaxation come over him as though his body and mind were telling him that the last vestiges of his life would soon escape his body and he would join his comrades in their silence. Feeling weaker and growing more faint, unable to move his own body due to his wound and the dead body that seemed to weigh heavier on him with each passing moment, Otto began to accept his coming fate.

He shifted his body as best he could to gain some portion of comfort. The dead body slipped a little downward but seemed to get caught on something. Otto noticed sticking out from under one side of the deceased's head was his silver belt buckle which had the inscription, "Gott mit uns." (God is with us).

Funny, he thought, how when something is part of your everyday uniform you tend to forget about it being there. Seeing the words calmed him. Slowly he lowered his head backward until it rested on the earth. A jolt of pain emitted from his leg and seemed to encase his whole body. He shuddered involuntarily. In his mind he began to pray.

"Have mercy on the souls of those dead who surround me, O Lord. I wish I could have done something to save them or provide comfort in their hour of death. Please accept them into your kingdom.

"Please provide comfort for those families who will learn of their loved one's deaths.

"Grant forgiveness to those of us who have killed. Accept us into your Kingdom so we may see our loved ones again.

"Holy Mary, mother of God, be with us sinners now and at the hour of our death."

He closed his eyes and pictured his exquisite Katarina and their four-year-old daughter Elke.

"Thank you, God, for blessing my life with them. Watch over them the rest of their lives. Please allow me to see them again in your heavenly home."

His final thoughts drifted with his soul above the continuing chaos of the battlefield.

Otto met all of them within minutes of entering heaven.

The first of the three soldiers was the one who had died in his arms. "I am Paul Kretschmer," he introduced himself with a bubbling amount of glee. "At the moment of my death, you were there for me, asking God to cleanse my soul."

"I am Peter Harden," said the youngest of the three who couldn't have been more than seventeen. "Thank you for asking God to bless me while you suffered through your fate."

The last of the trio hugged him before speaking to him. "I am Werner Messers. Your kindness at the hour of our death on our behalf will always be appreciated. My parents were comforted in knowing that I did not die alone and that you prayed for us. A witness to your final moments relayed to them what happened."

Otto was very taken back by the plaudits being showered on him. He couldn't figure out how someone moments from their own death could have done so many things to help others.

"Don't look so stunned," the sweet voice of his Katarina sounded forth. The sight of her and Elke, holding her hand, melted his emotions. He wrapped one arm around her while scooping little Elke up with his other. "I know the war sometimes shook your convictions," Katarina said, "but I know you never lost your faith in our God. You are a good man, Otto. God is always with us. Even when I received word of your death, and I anguished for years and years, I knew we would be together again."

Elke playfully tugged at Otto's ear. "You told me, Daddy, that God is always with us and when we talk with Him he always hears us."

Otto smiled at the wisdom of his young child. He suddenly realized how wholesome and pure his body felt. The air smelled clean, reminding him of a freshly bathed and powdered baby. It was a new life, one he was ready to embrace with all of his heart, his mind, and his soul. In that instant he realized how beautiful heaven was going to be for everyone who would be joining him as the wonders of the Grand Reunion continued to play out.

It never crossed Otto's mind to think about what might happen to those who would not be granted access to the home of the Creator.

39

He had slept soundly through the night. It was only when he awoke from his slumber and attempted to navigate through the wakening hours of the day that life became less than tolerable. There was never a way to escape from the repetitive cycle.

The war returned to him as his eyelids rose.

"As events progressed that day, machine gunners opened up on us from two angles and in an instant three of my friends who I had known since grammar school were killed, their bodies chopped up like meat in a butcher's shop. I fell on top of one of them and then burrowed behind him for safety. I could feel the bullets thud into his body while I lay with my face snug against his back. Over the course of the next several hours I could feel the warmth of his body slowly cool as life drained from him. My senses overlapped one another. I could see the crimson fluid of life leak from the holes the bullets had made in him as it was absorbed by his dirt brown shirt. The clamor of war continued as I experienced my own personal breakdown. The melodious, disgusting odor of death ingrained itself into my memory. I would carry that with me every waking moment of my existence. All my life if I saw the color red I would think about poor Creighton lying there and dying while I did nothing to help him, instead I hid behind him to save my own life. The color brown reminded me of his uniform filled with bullet holes. Whenever I looked upon a field of splendid green grass I thought back to that small patch of green that we had just trampled across before the German gunners zeroed in on my pals and began shredding them. How they missed me I can't understand. Everything in my life took me back there. Every day of my life I went back there. Any noise reminded me of the staccato of the machine guns or the explosion of hand grenades or shells. It just never left my head, except when I was sleeping. I never had a dream or a nightmare while I slept. The only way I could face each day was by sleeping as long as I could. How do you hold a job down when anything you do reminds you of your pals being killed in front of your eyes in such a barbaric way? Even sitting on a bench in a peaceful park reminded me of visiting their graves after the war and even then I could hear their voices asking me to save them and help them as they laid there with bullets in them and they were dying and I just cowered behind them trying to make myself safe just wanting to live and get back home was all I wanted at that moment."

The angel listening to the young Canadian emote his feelings at the pace of a courthouse stenographer allowed him to finish before offering a response. The angel had great empathy for Hamilton Ashton, who at the age of twenty had been a participant in Canadian lore what is known as the Battle of Vimy Ridge. In one sense it was a unique battle where a young nation had come together to earn its acceptance among the armies of the world. It helped forge the national identity and establish the reputation of determination, dependability, and toughness of Canada's sons.

In another sense, the battle wasn't any different from almost every other battle which had taken place during the war. Thousands of young men from opposing armies were killed on the once beautiful fields of the French countryside while thousands and thousands and thousands more were physically maimed or, as witnessed in the case of Hamilton Ashton, mentally maimed for the remainder of their natural lives.

As he finished his last sentence and took a deep breath in preparation of launching into another rambling soliloquy, the angel placed a comforting hand on his shoulder and placed his index finger on Hamilton's lips to signal him to stay silent.

"You're in heaven, child. You will only know happiness in God's house."

Hamilton closed his eyes in relief. His body went from rigid tenseness to a noticeable relaxed state in a matter of moments. His peacefulness was interrupted by a friendly tone.

"I've been looking all day for you, pal."

Hamilton's eyelids slowly rose to reveal the image of his long lost friend, Creighton.

His emotions churned. "I'm so sorry, Cray," he began with the tears already blurring his vision and the image of his friend. "You saved my life that day at Vimy. I've waited all my life to thank you. I'm so sorry for using you that way, that was so wrong of me. I'm sorry."

"It's okay. It's okay," Creighton said. "I was happy to be able to do something to help you stay alive." He continued to comfort his dear friend, "There's no more sadness. We're home now, for good. Everything and everyone here is well. We've suffered and we've waited long enough for this moment. It's time for us to celebrate life."

40

William Johnstone Milne sat patiently waiting for his boys to come greet him. Born in Scotland but moving to Saskatchewan in 1910, he ended up serving with the 16th Infantry Battalion as part of the Canadian Expeditionary Force that, like thousands of others, would make their mark for posterity at the Battle of Vimy Ridge.

As the conflict raged, Milne observed the location of German machine guns wreaking destruction on the men of his unit as they forged forward. Crawling across the battlefield on his hands and knees, Milne not only killed the hostile machine gun crew but captured the gun and used it to provide covering fire for his advancing comrades. A short time later, he replicated his earlier feat as the valiant Canadians approached another line of German fortifications. His actions not only showcased his bravery but his affection for his fellow soldiers. They were his boys, as he liked to refer to them since most were younger than him, who at the ripe old age of twenty four-had become a big brother to many of those still in their teens or early twenties.

He sat there thinking of them as he had last seen them, alive, with the vigor and fervor of youth.

Despite Milne's bravery, he, and they, had all died that day.

John Erskine Clark Milliken, who Milne called "King Milliken," always joking with him that any man with four names had to be the member of a royal family, not some lowly private serving time in a trench somewhere on the fringes of No Man's Land.

Alexander Mitchell, who only wanted to spend the mornings fishing and the evenings hunting back home in his beloved Canadian wilderness.

Albert Baldwin, the best soldier of the group, which didn't make any difference as they advanced forward into the unending phalanx of machine gun bullets coming from the German lines.

Nathan Payne, who Milne saw get killed, falling forward with blood distorting his handsome features that so many French ladies had swooned over when they spent leave time in Paris.

George Moore, who in his innocence of youth couldn't figure out why Canada was fighting in the war but knew he didn't want to miss being part of an event that would define the lives of his generation for all time.

Alfred Morison, who could run faster than anyone he had ever seen in his life.

Cedric Johnson, an individual of unquestionable character. He had confided to Milne that he was entertaining thoughts of becoming a priest after the war in order to balance the violence his life had been exposed to during their time in France.

Lost in thought he didn't see his boys approaching. Happiness descended upon him with great velocity. They had noticed him first and their passion upon sighting him led them into running toward him with such joy and abandon that they couldn't stop themselves from knocking him over.

None of them had realized how close they were to a nearby pond which was now transformed from a scene of idyllic serenity to one of chaotic excitement. "King" Milliken and Cedric had reached Milne first and wrapped their arms around him as though tackling him. As they rolled into the lily pad filled water, the others just kept following, letting their emotions take charge of their actions. Soon they were all in the pond jumping about, splashing one another, dunking one another under the floating leaves of green, laughing and smiling and enjoying the moment. Once what was denied them, now they basked in the glory of their youth.

41

Corporal Freddie Stowers was only twenty-one years old when he performed his act of heroism that saved the lives of so many of his fellow soldiers and friends of the 371st Infantry Regiment. He came from Sandy Springs, South Carolina, another of the endless towns strung across America in the early 1900s where the ugliness of racial segregation denied so many people in society the wondrous experience of getting to know their fellow neighbors and citizens. These were the consequences of simple hatred based on exterior judgment of one another due to fear, learned ignorance, and a self-ishness of the soul.

Despite the inequality faced by himself, his brothers in arms throughout the 93rd Infantry Division, and his family back in the United States, Freddie continued to be an example to all who knew him as the type of person who put others first, symbolizing the great strength others recognize in individuals of admirable character.

His Congressional Medal of Honor Citation would read:

> *A few minutes after the attack began (on Hill 188 in the Champagne Marne Sector, France), the enemy ceased firing and began climbing up onto the parapets of the trenches, holding up their arms as if wishing to surrender. The enemy's actions caused the American forces to cease fire and to come out into the open. As the company started forward and when within 100 meters of the trench line, the*

enemy jumped back into their trenches and greeted Corporal Stowers's company with interlocking bands of machine gun fire and mortar fire causing well over fifty percent casualties. Faced with incredible enemy resistance, Corporal Stowers took charge, setting such a courageous example of personal bravery and leadership that he inspired his men to follow him in the attack.

With extraordinary heroism and complete disregard of personal danger under devastating fire, he crawled forward leading his squad toward an enemy machine gun nest, which was causing heavy casualties to his company. After fierce fighting, the machine gun position was destroyed and the enemy soldiers were killed. Displaying great courage and intrepidity, Corporal Stowers continued to press the attack against a determined enemy. While crawling forward and urging his men to continue the attack on a second trench line, he was gravely wounded by machine gun fire. Although, Corporal Stowers was mortally wounded, he pressed forward, urging on the members of his squad, until he died.

The first one to meet Freddie in heaven was the man who had been his commanding officer during the war, Colonel P. L. Miles. Always one for being serious and formal, Miles couldn't resist gathering up as many members of the old division almost upon his arrival through the pearly gates, and preparing a sumptuous feast for the man who defined the spirit and humanity typical of all those who had served in the 371st Infantry Regiment.

The whole event was physically and emotionally overwhelming. His whole regiment was there. They mobbed Freddie as the hero he was in their eyes, minds, and hearts. While two and three at a time shook his hand, others slapped his back with warm gestures of appreciation and love. Those he had seen killed in front of him and around him that September day were flashing him smiles, telling him how much they appreciated his bravery, and how happy they were to all be home as one big family again.

Those who he had saved that day by his selfless actions hugged him individually and with great passion, each blessing him with verbal praises that echoed the same sentiment over and over again, that because of his actions, they lived not only that day but through the remaining three months of the war as well, returning to the arms of their families and living long lives because of his actions.

When he reached the end of the line, Freddie turned around looking for his old colonel once again. Wiping the emotions from his eyes, and speaking with the dignity that was his hallmark, he inquired, "Colonel Miles, I am very thankful for seeing all of you again, and I can't put into proper words what your thoughts for me by you and the men are doing to my emotions, and no disrespect to any of you, but can you tell me if the Germans, if those men I killed that day, are they here also? I would like to converse with them for a while and get to know them."

The old officer offered up a look that showed understanding and admiration. "I expected nothing less from you, Freddie. I took the liberty of inviting those soldiers to dine with all of us later this evening. Every one of them said that they would be here and that they are anxious to meet you and share their friendship with you. I think all of us are going to have a beautiful and enjoyable time up here."

42

Entrance into heaven was especially apprehensive for the man whose world-famous literary alter ego was known as Sherlock Holmes. Receiving news that his beloved son Kingsley Doyle was wounded during the Battle of the Somme had stirred emotions in the talented writer that he found hard to describe in any written format. There was some solace after the initial shock, however, in realizing that a wounded child was still an alive child, something that millions of parents had already experienced by the midpoint of the war. However, as millions more would eventually discover, the enemies of life during wartime had many ways of winning victories over the living. When Arthur Conan Doyle received notification that Kingsley was dead due to complications from influenza obtained while recovering from his wounds, he was devastated in a way that would consume the rest of his living days on earth.

So emotionally distraught at life without Kingsley, Arthur soon embraced the world of spiritualism in a desperate attempt to make some type of contact with his son from beyond the grave. While the desires of some spiritualists were genuine, there were empathetic mediums who conducted séances so grieving loved ones could find some sense of relief at knowing their deceased family members were on the other side, safe and secure from any more worldly pain, they were far and few in between. After the war, Arthur had attended a number of sessions where he was led to believe Kingsley did communicate with him and assured him all was well with him in the spirit world. Yet afterward, in the privacy of his own pain and household, Arthur continued to question whether he would ever truly see Kingsley again, let alone make any type of spiritual contact with him.

A friend of Arthur's who also lost his son in the war summed it up this way. "You're just lonely all the time. Even with your wife in the house, she would be mourning in her own way, and I in my own way. There wasn't a lot of talking because it would always lead to more tears and you just couldn't go about your day crying all the time. Instead, we went about our day in quiet, somber ways. Death seemed to be more of a constant companion than life."

Arthur wasn't within the gates of heaven more than fifteen minutes when he laid eyes on his beloved Kingsley. Arthur was so overcome with elation that he couldn't speak, but the smile which he flashed illuminated his face for the first time since Kingsley's death was all that his son needed to see in order to feel fulfilled. They remained embraced for such a long time that they almost seemed to be one individual instead of two separate. When they allowed some space between them, Kingsley spoke first.

"I knew you were trying to reach me, Father. All those years that went by. I knew it was punishing for you, not hearing from me, not knowing where I was. But I found out that's the way it works on this side. Once we're here, we're not allowed to cross back over."

Arthur looked his son over and hugged him again, perhaps even harder this time around than their initial embrace. "My life lost direction after you died, my dear son. I never doubted you were here. I needed to hear your voice one more time. It was just so empty without you."

"That won't be an issue anymore. I know since being here that our hearts are fulfilled with God's love. We're home now, together again. I love you, Father."

43

He sat behind his large mahogany desk looking out over his new world.

In the front of the room the desks were aligned in perfect rows four across and five deep. A strange inner feeling influenced him to stand up and make his way to the rows of orderly inanimate objects. He soon found himself shuffling the desks around until they were in circular groups of five. This made him feel better, and more relaxed. They no longer reminded him of lifeless wooden soldiers waiting for orders.

Walking to the back of the room he smiled in approval at the large drawing tables where the students would be able to pursue their creative talents. The accouterments of imagination filled the nearby shelves. Crayons, markers, and paints showcasing hundreds of shades of color seemed to be in endless supply. Papers of all shapes, sizes, width, and thickness occupied dozens of cubbies. Baskets filled with an array of cutting and designing scissors were filled to the brim. Sketch tablets and every type of drawing utensil filled up the cabinets making up the last row of the massive storage unit.

It filled him with the inspiration to educate young minds and bring their imagination to reality in a way that they could appreciate their lives.

A tear irritated his vision as he thought back to those ghastly days during the war when he spent day after day teaching young men how to kill and destroy humanity. Being a drill sergeant was a mixed blessing. He was safe from the horrors of the frontlines but being a man of conscience he spent many sleepless nights trying to figure out if he was any different from the soldier who killed another soldier in combat.

During drill, it was easy to put on the facade of the tough, no-nonsense officer whose job it was to prepare kids in their late teens and early twenties the intricacies of killing other humans. His was a job of dehumanization in order to make efficient soldiers in the art of destroying the enemy.

His words haunted him in the throes of his nightly slumber.

"Twist his neck to the left, and draw the blade of your knife across his neck going in the opposite direction."

"When you bayonet the enemy, stick it in and twist it to maximize the internal damage. Then push up and pull out, sometimes that will bring with it some of the organs you are filleting and it will speed up the death of your enemy, in case you wanted to be a little humane to the sorry bastard."

"Aim for the middle of the enemy's chest, if you shoot high, then you'll hit him in the face. Either way is a good way for you to stop that sonuvabitch in his tracks."

"Don't worry about the cries of agony coming from the enemy after you shot him. That could be you lying there instead. Your job is to kill the enemy, not have mercy for him."

He woke up most nights trembling. A man who thinks a lot with nowhere to go in the early hours of the morning can torture himself to the point of self destruction. The reality was he had mercy for other people who happened to be soldiers, and deep in his heart knew that he could never kill another human. In his private sanctuary, he couldn't rationalize being so enthusiastic and cold hearted in teaching others to kill.

When did a dream become a nightmare?

The innocence of the young recruits was seen on all of their faces. He was the killer of their childhood. His day consisted of doing everything he could to convince them why and show them how to kill the other young boys of the opposing nations. He felt satisfaction in seeing a young recruit on the target range score a bull's-eye from a hundred yards away; he had helped to hone that skill that lie within that young man who had never had a rifle in his hand his entire life.

When the bodies of the young Australians and New Zealanders he had helped train started to come back home in coffins to be buried in their towns and villages throughout the lands, he became more despondent at night, though more ruthless in his training sessions of new recruits the following day. It was another one of the endless ways war scarred the life of the individual.

His conscience questioned him daily. He had never been to Europe. He had never met a German or a Turk. Why was he so intent on making sure they were killed in prodigious numbers in the most proficient ways by the boys he trained? Was he doing something immoral or his just duty to his country? How would he reconcile his life before God on the day of final judgment?

The answers he sought remained elusive the rest of his days. He lived into his seventies before ironically peacefully passing away one night in the midst of a restful sleep.

When he entered heaven that morning of the first day of The Grand Reunion, he was at peace with himself and all of humanity. Jesus had met him along with others who had been drill instructors of other armies during the war, and they were absolved of any wrongdoing or perceived wrongdoing on their part. His private tribulations experienced throughout his life more than made up for any pretense of penance that many might think would be imposed upon him by the Creator. Those truly accountable for the killed and dead of the war would be dealt with in God's own good time.

As he walked back to the front of the classroom, his new classroom, he sat back down in the chair behind the teacher's desk and smiled thinking of and looking forward to the coming days where he would enjoy teaching the children in heaven about all the wondrous creative talents that they had bottled up inside of them. There would be great pleasure in helping them to unlock the beauty of their dynamic imaginations while using his true talents for the benefit of everyone.

He realized he was calm and at peace with himself. It's all he ever wanted in life, and now it was his to share and enjoy while contributing to a positive impact on the lives of so many others.

44

The war made them haggard. Endless months of combat that stretched into years had killed their friends and countrymen by the hundreds of thousands for nothing. Those who had survived from one day to the next were physically worn out, their bodies no longer able to contribute anything positive to their existence.

The war went on. The lies from their leaders continued unabated. Those who had not an inkling of what they were doing to a generation of humanity proceeded to delude themselves that each next big battle or each next big push would be the one to end the war. They were oblivious to the pain they inflicted upon their own armies because they no longer saw them as individuals who were capable of thinking for themselves. They believed them to be loyal soldiers without individual characteristics who would continue to obey delusional orders steeped in ignorance that continued to appease Satan's appetite.

In the trenches, underneath woven linen which maintained nationalistic segregated identities as much as No Man's Land and endless tangles of barbed wire created physical barriers, the hearts, minds, and souls of the soldiers yearned to be human again. Many began thinking about if there really was any legitimate reason to go kill those young men in the opposing trench who they believed to be just like themselves.

The French attack known as the Second Battle of the Aisne in April 1917 led to another one hundred thousand dead and maimed for life physically, mentally, and emotionally young men, the last of the cream of France's youth for another generation. Those who survived the first week of the failed offensive were expected to charge forward again when flippantly ordered to do so again by those who chose to keep the bloodletting continuously in flux.

"When men taking a stand to claim and assert their rights as people once again refused to obey orders like sheep anymore, they were denounced as mutineers and traitors," wrote Francois Allard in his last letter to his parents, the night before he and dozens of others were executed for their actions of conscience.

Remy Marchand tried to explain to his wife in his last letter how those in command did their best to minimize his status as a person of free thought. "They told me by not obeying orders and attacking the enemy that I had betrayed the sacred honor of France. I inquired of them whether or not I counted for anything. Did I, Remy Marchand, matter? Was I obsolete as an individual?"

Remy and Francois were shot to death by firing squad, as well as dozens more, simply because the government could not execute the estimated one hundred thousand other French troops who also refused to charge forward to their deaths after the debacle at Aisnes. They entered through heaven's gates together and exchanged joyous greetings. They shared a genuine desire to meet the others who had suffered and shared their fate in order to enjoy that moment of bliss they had thought about moments prior to being killed by their own government.

It wasn't long before they were meeting other French soldiers such as Gregoir Bissette and Xavier Moreau, two others who had been chosen at random to be made examples of for the others who dare question military and political power during a time of war. They all agreed that they had made the right decision in speaking their minds and claiming their individual sense of dignity and humanity during those sad, dark days. What brightened their spirits even more were meeting with those soldiers who had carried out their executions.

Jerome Charron was one of the members of the firing squad which had executed Remy. He shook Remy's hand while apologizing for being weak and not standing up to those who had ordered him to enforce their will upon the soldiers as a whole. Remy not only shook his hand but hugged him as well, telling him there was nothing to apologize for.

"All of us were weak," Remy told him. "From the start of the war, when we should have stood up and denied those who governed over us the power to wage war with our lives, we gave in to evil, and for our weakness we were justly punished."

While Jerome wept, half out of sadness for his earthly mistakes and half tears of joy for being home in heaven, another person approached Remy and Francois to thank them for actions related to the so-called mutiny.

"I am Pierre Laurent," the young man presented himself. "Thank you for speaking out on our behalf. I lacked the courage to do so. I am sad to say that what I was happy about most was that my name was not one of those randomly selected to be executed. It was only after you were dead that I began to think for myself and realize that you and the others stood up for something that truly mattered." Remy and Francois listened with great respect as he continued to evoke his thoughts. "The questions you posed to those in authority made them think if only for a few seconds, about what was truly being accomplished by their unrelenting determination to keep the war in motion. Surely, I believe, those who were responsible for the suffering of our generation will be held accountable."

Remy smiled nervously, not sure what to say. "Thank you for your kind words," was all he could offer up. Francois stepped forward and embraced Pierre as well as Remy. "I think it is time for us to enjoy being here, and let God take care of those other issues that are not in our hands. Come on with me, all of you," he motioned with his head to the others, "I heard that the dining halls in heaven are everything we talked and dreamed about while we were in the trenches. Let us go and celebrate."

45

The amount of food being prepared and consumed throughout the banquet halls would overwhelm even the most dedicated statistician. After all an entire generation of humans were all here at the same time. As is the great gift of food, it helps to bring families and people together and is a crucial ingredient in the convening of loved ones and establishing a sense of community. The sharing of time as well as delectable delights breeds unity among those who partake in one of the greatest gifts of humankind.

The sweet aroma of fried onions next to a sizzling steak topped with green and red peppers melded with bits of sharp Vermont cheese would stop any doughboy in his tracks, especially one who had never been lucky enough to encounter such an aroma anywhere in France during his time in the old country. Sadly, part of the great adventure the Yanks encountered during the war was subsiding on canned meat and hard crackers, which some believed had been saved by the US government since the end of the Spanish–American War.

During his first day in heaven, however, Jason Anthony Visson of Clearwater, Florida, was enjoying something more delectable than any type of epicurean delight that was being prepared in the St. Blaise Banquet Hall. He was engaged in a moment of pure bliss with an angel, at least in his mind an angel, he had first seen back in 1918. A short distance from the entryway to the dining hall, dressed in her white skirt and white blouse, topped off with a white hat and a little Red Cross pin, stood Rachel Brown, all five foot two inches of her.

It was the same outfit she wore in France while she was a member of the Red Cross.

"You are still the most beautiful sight I have seen in my life," the young man declared with great confidence in his voice.

Rachel smiled with equal enthusiasm while she continued to hand out warm, freshly made donuts to anyone who wanted one before they made their way into St. Blaise Banquet Hall.

"Get them while they're warm and fresh," she chirped. "Just the way you remember them back in the day," she interjected every other time she repeated her first line.

Jason couldn't hold back his excitement. "You were the first American gal I saw in France after being on that transport ship for days coming across the Atlantic. There you were, waiting for us with hot coffee and warm donuts as we came down the gangway. Nicer than walking on solid land instead of a swaying deck was the welcome aroma of fresh donuts and some hot java. I remember thinking coming off of that ship that it smells just like the United States over here. I thought for a moment the ship had turned around in the middle of the night and took us back to New York."

In the midst of a throng of arms reaching for a cinnamon or powdered treat, Rachel continued to entice those heading toward the banquet hall with its more exquisite fare. Almost all of those who stopped for a donut were the young boys and men who had served in France as part of Pershing's American Expeditionary Force. It seemed that only the Americans could appreciate the memory that a donut could stir up, even in heaven. For them, during the war, it was their first taste of home while being in a foreign land for the first time in their lives, and the kind gesture from the young American girls who had volunteered to come to France to offer them a reminder of being in mom's kitchen or at the neighborhood diner was something that remained with them all the days of their lives.

"Thank you for your kind words," Rachel offered up to him as she handed him a plate of the deep fried delectable delights.

Jason stood against a wooden chair that occupied some space next to the table where Rachel was placing fresh-baked donuts at a regular clip. While some of the boys never did pick up the nasty habit of smoking while in France, everyone who was there consumed Red Cross donuts by the dozen whenever the opportunity had presented itself.

"I saw you," Jason said as he bit into a new donut. "I saw your smile from a hundred yards away before I even got close to the tables where you were working. I got out of my line which was shorter and stood in the next line over which was twice as long so I could end up getting my donuts and coffee from you, just so I could say hi to you."

Rachel offered him a napkin to wipe the corner of his mouth which had some white powder on it which hadn't quite made it into his mouth. She thought it was cute how excited he was to be talking with her, but she kept it to herself and let him go on without interruption between bites and an occasional gulp of coffee.

"Do you remember me?" Jason asked in exaggerated exasperation between a swallow and a new bite.

"I assume you must have been one of the million or so doughboys who I had handed a donut to in France," she said with a tinge of sarcastic humor in her voice.

Jason threw his head back and then rolled it from side to side in disbelief. He placed his half-eaten plate of deep fried favorites and empty coffee mug on the table that separated the two of them. Just as he opened his mouth to speak again Rachel winked at him and smiled.

"Yes!" Jason shouted in glee. "I knew you recognized me, I knew it."

Rachel came around the table and the two of them embraced with such abandon that they almost fell to the ground.

"I didn't think you would be able to find me up here with so many people so after I entered the gates earlier this morning I decided to wear my Red Cross uniform from the war so you would recognize me. Some of the angels told me it was okay to wear since it wasn't a military uniform."

Jason stepped back from their embrace but he still kept his hands on Rachel's shoulders. "I knew I would know you the instant I laid eyes on you again. After we met in France I think you were the only person I thought about, next to my mom and pop back in the states. I saw them earlier this morning and they knew right away that I would go looking for you."

Rachel leaned forward and kissed him, the only way she could think of at that moment to get him to calm down and stop talking.

It worked.

When their lips receded from one another their eyes locked. Jason's heart was telling him his dream had been fulfilled, but he had to hear it from Rachel to verify that it was really true.

"We're never going to be apart again, are we, honey?"

"Nothing will ever separate us," Rachel said with loving confidence. "I've held you in my heart all these years, Jason, from the time we first met to caring for you while you were wounded in the field hospital, and being next to you when you passed."

Jason was stunned. In the euphoria of the proceedings of the day including seeing Rachel, he had forgotten all about the events which followed their initial encounter after landing in France. Once Rachel brought it up, however, they came flooding back with intensity.

"After I talked to you and we went on our way, we trained for a few weeks and then they moved us up to the trenches. The first day I was in the lines we were shelled by the Germans. I never knew what it was that hit me in the face but that was the last time I saw the daylight of life."

Rachel picked up the story of the last days of Jason's life.

"I was at the hospital tent when I saw them bringing you in. They hadn't bandaged your face yet so I recognized you immediately. From the distance I was standing I could see the burn marks to both of your eyes and I began to feel a pain in my chest. It was a throbbing, gnawing pain which I had never experienced before in my life. I knew I was hurting for you. I know it sounds like romanticized drivel, but that's when I knew those feelings I felt for you when we first met were true feelings that would only have existed if I had love for you."

Jason smiled. He found hearing the story comforting.

"I don't remember you being with me when I died. What happened?"

Rachel became emotional as she recalled the scene in her mind before relaying it to Jason. "You never regained consciousness from when they brought you in but I knew I couldn't let you lay there and die alone. They let me sit next to your cot for the next two days as your situation worsened but there was nothing they could do to reverse what was happening. I sat holding your hand the whole time imagining what everything would have been like for us if we would have been married after the war."

Jason hesitated to ask but his curiosity had to be satisfied. "Am I correct in assuming you never got married, that you lived the rest of your life single?"

Rachel gripped Jason's hands and squeezed them tight. "I have believed all my life that there are things that God plans for us and that having faith in those plans, especially when we don't understand them, is a way we reaffirm our belief in his divinity. I lived another fifty-seven years after you died that day, and I don't believe that that is actually a long time to wait in order to spend my life in eternity with you."

Their love which had been born in the all-too brief moments that the Great War had allotted them, and the faith they had in the love that they were blessed with, which began the first moments they encountered one another, would now be enjoyed by them for all of the ages.

46

A sizeable gathering of people was to be found in The Grove of St. James and St. John, also known as The Brothers Grove by the locals who were there before the influx of the World War I generation. Not only veterans of the war constantly made their way into the site but many were bringing their family members as well. British and German mixed side by side as they entered the grove with an air of anticipation and excitement that could be felt by all present. They had waited a lifetime to meet the Angel of Mons, as they had always referred to him since first setting eyes upon this heavenly host back in the early days of the war in August 1914.

Private Albert Smith of the Royal Fusiliers had gone to his death with the comfort of knowing he would be reunited in heaven with his family and loved ones. He was there that night that soldiers on both sides of the battlefield saw the apparition appear in the sky high above the earliest No Man's Land of the Great War. Holding the hand of his wife and young child, he told them of his experience.

"I was wounded shortly after seeing the angel. His presence was calming for as much as all of us were shocked by what we were seeing. He didn't speak to us but you could feel his message resonate from within your soul. I knew in that instant that everything was going to be alright, that even if I died, which I did the very next day, and as I lay there bleeding to death, I wasn't in any pain. I knew that we would all be together again here, as we are now."

Another young man strode aside Albert and his family wearing the same look of anticipation on his face as that displayed by

Albert. When they bumped shoulders they quickly apologized to one another but when their eyes met they had that feeling that they had met once before. Recognizing this, Albert started to say, "I know you—" but was cut off by, "You are the Tommy I killed the day after seeing the angel." He couldn't get any further as his words became mixed with sobs.

Albert let go of his wife's and child's hands and wrapped both of them around the young German's shoulders in a huge bear hug. "It's okay," he whispered to him, "it's okay. We are here together again, and here there is only happiness."

The German recovered his emotions and held his hand out to Albert. "My name is Jozef Hulbrecht. I was part of the 1st German Army, but I am happy that that is no longer how I identify myself."

A few feet away from them stood another pair of former enemies sharing their eagerness to come face to face with the Angel on Mons.

"When I first saw the image appearing in the night sky, it was as though I could feel my body empty of any hatred that it had stored up over my first eighteen years of life," said Andrew Callahan, who was a private of the Royal Fusiliers, actually serving in the same company of Albert Smith.

"I had the same experience," said Emil Prust. "I had always wanted to be a soldier for the Kaiser as a little boy growing up in Prussia. But that night at Mons, after seeing our angel, I began to feel that there was more to life than learning how to kill one another. It no longer made sense, and I began to wonder why I had always gained so much pleasure in killing someone who was my enemy, only because I was educated to see them as my enemy."

They stood there with arms wrapped around each other's shoulders as old friends who had not seen each other for a long period of time tend to do once they are reunited. Their attention was drawn to the glowing light on the horizon of the grove which began to rise a little higher in the sky as it came closer to where they were standing. In a short period of time, the murmuring from the crowd had silenced itself and such as it was the first time so long ago, the Angel of Mons was once again hovering above them.

This time, though, it was vastly different.

Now, they were thousands of young men meeting together not in a state of loathing, hatred, and conflict but in solemnity and brotherly love. Their identities were as individuals, not as an artificial uniformed entity brought together to annihilate.

"I felt since I mesmerized you so much with my appearance in 1914 that I would do it again for old time's sake," the Angel of Mons announced with some wry sarcasm in his voice. His adoring audience filled the air with joyous laughter. After all, it was an occasion of happiness.

As the laughter faded, the angel descended from the sky and sat down on a small canvas folding chair reminiscent of those used by soldiers on both sides of the trenches during the conflict. Situated on a small hillock he could easily be viewed by everyone present. The ten thousand or so who had come to see their real life apparition from the days of their youth squatted down on their haunches or sat cross-legged on the cool, but comfortable fields of alluring emerald shaded grass.

"For many of you, this is your first time together since you were killed at the Battle of Mons. I know the joy you are experiencing today is immeasurable. To see old comrades, and family members who suffered for years and decades after the war due to your absence, is a sensation that you will enjoy for all days forever. To see old enemies, and not feel that human weakness of hate that was inflicted upon your consciousness by those of weak fortitude, and misguided lapses of power, is your heavenly reward for having endured the evil that was cast upon you in your earthly existence."

Hearty cheers greeted the uplifting words of the angel.

"Through the dark moments of your youth you held steadfast in your true faith and beliefs, and when you sought the presence of God he sent me as a reminder that you were heard and not forgotten. As his own Son suffered in his earthly form, so you suffered and endured what God set aside for you. His blessings are now bestowed upon you as long as you dwell in His house, and as what was offered to you earlier today, once again you are welcomed home."

This time there were fewer cheers, mainly due to so many using their hands to wipe away the tears of joy which overcame so many who had endured so much despair and deprivation from the earliest days of the war. Without any fanfare, the Angel of Mons departed from the scene in order to visit all those others who had seen him throughout the course of the horrible conflict. While his original contact with soldiers in the earliest days of the war was more famously known, an endless amount of soldiers had similar occurrences over the course of the war. The Angel of Mons would be spending many, many days reuniting with those who knew what they saw amidst man's best destructive effort to convince them otherwise. Their beliefs were proof that their faith was more powerful than words of hatred spewed forth by propaganda posters or the destruction of human bodies by Krupp steel or the Waltham Abbey Royal Gunpowder Mills.

47

A short distance from the entrance to The Grove of St. James and St. John sat a forlorn figure whose conscience was getting the best of him even though he had been granted entrance into heaven. Like everyone else he had been overwhelmed by the emotions of the grand welcome and march through the pearly gates as well as the euphoria of seeing those loved ones he had not seen for years in between their deaths and his eventual own demise in 1989 at the age of ninety-seven.

With those feelings having diminished a degree throughout the course of the day, Adam Cosgrove had started to question, as many others were doing as we have already seen, why they had been allowed into heaven despite what they had done with their life on earth. Unable to serve in a military capacity due to a childhood accident which led to him having his left foot amputated, he spent the war utilizing his creative talents working as part of the Propaganda Ministry. Sitting in a comfortable office sometimes up to ten or twelve hours a day, he sketched, drew, or painted everything from handbills dropped from airplanes over enemy lines encouraging German soldiers to surrender to full-size posters which demonized the Huns as the destroyers of all that was civilized and good in the world. On a slow day, he would sit around with others in the office and shape new slogans to encourage the folks on the home front to keep supporting the war effort especially by encouraging more young boys and men to join the military in order to replace those who were killed in the early battles.

His long life had been one of great emotional conflict.

Much as he looked in the days of his youth, with the exception that now his body was without flaw, Adam sat alongside a small stream that quietly flowed past him, its calmness helping to steady the anxiety he felt growing within him. He reached forward and scooped a palm full of water that he quickly splashed across the back of his neck. It was so refreshing that he repeated the event in order to enjoy the sensation one more time.

"One of my favorite places to rest," the soft, self-assured voice greeted him from across the stream.

Stunned by his presence, Adam was at a loss for words and could only blurt out, "My God."

"No," he was gently corrected, "that would be my Father. I'm Jesus. I know we look alike, but trust me I'm the son, not the father."

Adam smiled sheepishly, a tad embarrassed.

"What troubles you?" Jesus asked in a tone that made Adam feel comfortable enough to begin opening up to him.

"I assume you know what I did with my life, especially during the war." He leaned forward to cup another handful of water but this time drank it instead of using it to cool the outside of his body. Jesus allowed him the moment to regain his thoughts.

"Your Father gave me the talent to draw and create, and I used it to convince young boys and men to go join the army, even after the Somme battle." He stopped himself and took a long, deep breath then began reciting the slogans which he had originated and included on his posters to encourage the population to support and participate in the war.

"Your King and Country Need You!"

"Join the Army until the War is Over."

Anger filled his voice. It was as though he was trying to denounce the works of his youth as a way of exorcising the guilt which he still felt even though he had already been granted acceptance into the home of Jesus's father.

"Britishers—Enlist To-Day."

"England Expects Every Man to do His Duty."

"Rally Round the Flag—We Must Have More Men."

He hung his head in shame.

"Wasted talent," he managed to barely whisper. "Your Father blessed me with great ability and unique aptitude, and I besmirched it in the name of empty nationalism and manufactured hatred."

Jesus strode across the stream and sat next to him.

"Did you believe the words you wrote when creating your works of propaganda?" he asked in a tone that did not accuse or judge.

Adam kept his head down and shrugged. "It became easier to hate the more I created slogans and painted posters. Early in the war I was angry that I couldn't serve in the front lines because of my leg injury. My friends convinced me that what I was doing was helping with the war effort, that it was important and that what I was doing made a difference. It became so easy to draw the lines and mix the paints and rhyme the words that created the images that motivated others to keep fighting."

Jesus remained quiet and let him speak at will. It was not his way to interrupt one of his children when they were in the midst of confessing their acts of ill will.

"It never registered with me the harm I had done until after the war was over and I began to see pictures of the dead and the devastation of the battlefields up close and personal. I mean, I saw pictures in the newspapers and films at the cinema during the course of the war, but it just seemed so easy to accept until I stood where they had died."

He closed his eyes and saw the sights that had caused such devastation to his psyche.

"I visited France a year after it all ended. It was in the vicinity of the Somme battlefield. The landscape was still decimated. We were told to be extra careful because there was still so much unexploded ammunition lying around and we were told we would be sightseeing at our own risk. I was walking in one of the trenches and I bent down to pick up a rather nice looking timepiece whose face was barely peeking out from under the semi-dry mud. When I tugged on it to loosen it from the soil I also extricated the arm that it was still attached to . . . just an arm. The rest of whoever it was just wasn't anywhere to be found.

"At that moment my mind started to think that that was my fault. All those boys who signed up to fight the Hun, those pals from all those towns who grew up together as childhood friends, whole groups were slaughtered in moments."

Adam openly wept.

"They were there because of my handiwork. My stupid, senseless posters that encouraged them to be men when they weren't men. I helped to kill all those boys as much as any German machine gunner."

"What did you do after the war with your talents?" Jesus asked him in a rather solemn tone.

Adam sniffled.

It pained him to say it.

"I did nothing.

"I drank away my guilt.

"Every time I saw someone who lost an arm, or a leg, or their eyesight, or their face, or their mind in the war, I'd turn away from them. I couldn't stand to look at the suffering that I had contributed to or see the pain that was a result of my influencing handiwork."

Another deep sigh emitted from Adam.

"All those years of life that you gave me . . . I was so lonely."

"You suffered for your choices more than most individuals," Jesus firmly stated with an air of authority that Adam knew meant that he had just been absolved of any wrongdoing.

"Thank you, Lord," Adam said with overwhelming sincerity as he clasped the hands of Jesus.

"You will never be asked to betray your talents for ill will again," Jesus declared. "Seek out the members of your family and revel in their company. Your life of despair was a great burden on them and they are looking forward to having those years with you back to enjoy this time around. Welcome, once again, to the house of my Father."

48

The flames shot high into the air with such ferocity behind them that it seemed to express their desire to burn the linens which fed their energy as quickly as possible. As the orange-red tongues whipped about, the sweet aroma of fresh hickory, the starter pieces of the enormous conflagration, mixed with the variety of predominantly wool and cotton fabrics being fed into the fire by a never-ending parade of angels.

Bells ringing throughout the far reaches of God's heavenly kingdom had signified a short time earlier that the ceremony known from previous reunions as the "burning of the uniforms" had commenced. They had been gathered from each of those entering through the pearly gates when they first arrived. Many had come to heaven wearing what they were last wearing when they were killed on the battlefields or had perished beneath the waters and seas of the earth. The angels who met them had quietly explained to them that the wearing of uniforms in heaven was not only prohibited but not necessary since everyone here would be seen and accepted as unique individuals of equal stature and no longer be defined by the artificial and manmade delusional labels of nationality or rank which only festered division and rancor.

The choice of what to wear that was offered up by the heavenly hosts included fashions of endless style, design, colors, fabrics, and even different time eras if one was so inclined from the World War I generation to see what they might look like wearing something from the time Jesus walked the earth up until the present twenty-first century. The only common thread all modes of dress shared is that none of them were in any way militaristic in nature or symbolism (The only outfit that raised potential controversy was the kilt worn by the Scots during the war. As long as they displayed no military decal, insignia, or color swatch associated with any specific military unit they were angel-approved wear in heaven). Many did prefer the free flowing white robes synonymous with that worn by Jesus, but the infinite variety of tastes possessed by each person contributed to a kaleidoscope of images that showcased an unending mosaic of free will.

German field gray and British tan khaki, Canadian light brown and American Marine dress blues, Russian greenish khaki and French silk red pantaloons from early in the war, sea outfits of admirals of all nations and navy whites of dutiful sailors, were just some of the voluminous types and styles of uniforms from all nations that were cast into the ever growing flames. They were joined by the puttees worn by Yankee doughboys, the black high boots of the Cossacks, the slouch hats of the ANZACS and Aussies, the soft felt caps and kepis of enlisted men from all the belligerent nations worn early in the war before they gave way to helmets, which would also enter the flames once the heat was high enough to melt down the distinctive round helmets of the late-coming Americans as well as the menacing looking picklehaube worn by the Kaiser's armies in 1914.

Uniforms which once represented the empires of Austria-Hungary, Ottoman, and Romanov were consumed and materialized into ashes alongside Italian and Serbian and Croatian militia and state military outfits which represented all branches of all military units. Attached to many uniforms were the metal decorations nations had used to award their soldiers for the so-called heroic acts of killing their fellow man. While those presentations to individuals comforted the leaders of the governments who sent their youth to kill the youth of other nations, and in their minds justified the continuation of the meaningless slaughter, those men spent their remaining living years in quiet reflection on what it all meant.

The quiet Tennessean Alvin York, who had killed twenty-eight Germans and captured 132 more during the Meuse-Argonne offensive in 1918 quietly watched as his uniform, with medals attached, perished in the flames. It brought a certain feeling of cleansing to his soul to see the items that everyone associated with him as being the defining moment of his life, in which he ended up being praised and honored for his ability with a rifle to snuff out the life of fellow humans, were no more. His desire from that moment on was to locate those twenty-eight persons whose lives he ended that October day and seek forgiveness from them. All he wanted after that was to humbly ask God for a piece of land to farm and harvest and be allowed to enjoy the satisfaction of working the land for the benefit of others.

At the start of the ceremony, many who surrounded the bonfire began quietly singing one of the more famous ballads from the Great War. Among the crowd was Lena Gilbert Ford, who wrote the haunting words of "Keep the Home Fires Burning" in 1914. Despite an emotional lump in many of their throats, the words could still be plainly heard as they sang en masse.

> *They were summoned from the hillside,*
> *They were called in from the glen,*
> *And the country found them ready*
> *At the stirring call for men.*
> *Let no tears add to their hardships*
> *As the soldiers pass along,*
> *And although your heart is breaking,*
> *Make it sing this cheery song:*
>
> *Keep the Home Fires Burning,*
> *While your hearts are yearning.*
> *Though your lads are far away*
> *They dream of home.*
> *There's a silver lining*
> *Through the dark clouds shining,*
> *Turn the dark cloud inside out*
> *Till the boys come home.*

As emotions welled up and considering the enormous amount of souls present, it was safe to say that an ocean of tears was soon released. This time, however, it was a different type of emotion, one more of joyful sadness. Sad in the sense that the words stirred the memories of those first months of the war when people cheered as their posterity marched off to war without the slightest hint of reality at how many would not return. In their minds they questioned that time and wondered how they could have been so foolish and blind. Now, as a four score chorus of angels strummed the melody of the old song on golden layered harps, family members and friends seeing their loved ones with them again felt their hearts reignited with kindness, wisdom and love. The power and blessings of the Holy Spirit had descended upon all of them.

The warmth of the fire comforted those who surrounded the pyre. It was soothing to the soul as well as the body. The ceremony left no one doubting that they were truly home in the House of the Lord and, like Alvin York, who was now searching out those individuals whose paths crossed with his during the war, countless others would continue to embark on their own journeys of reconciliation and understanding.

49

Matthew Ryan hadn't stopped smiling for the past few hours even though his hands and fingers had tired themselves out from the constant petting and belly rubs they had performed over and over and over and over again on his beloved and faithful golden retriever, Holly. Matthew had left for the war from the small village of Lowville in upstate New York at the foot of the Adirondack region a week after he had graduated from the local high school academy in the spring of 1917. He joined the army before the nation had declared war on Germany, but he knew it was going to happen eventually so he figured why wait. Just as well, his grandfather had fought in the Civil War as a member of General Grant's Army that finished that dreadful conflict at Appomattox Court House in 1865 and Matthew had believed he owed it to the family name to serve on behalf of the country when the nation was in need.

Holly had been his birthday present four years earlier and as Matthew grew into his mid teens and young manhood, Holly was his everyday companion who provided unconditional love, moments of endless enjoyment and laughter, and in the cold northern New York winters, her seventy-pound body and thick coat of golden brown fur was like having an additional blanket on him at night after she crawled up into his bed and draped herself over him as they retired for the evening. In the mornings, Holly's licking of Matthew's face meant it was time for him to feed her and then begin their morning run.

It took them a while from the time Holly was a pup until she had grown and built up muscle and endurance but they eventually ran side by side the five miles that Matthew covered each day just as the sun was rising over the majestic farmland that was the face of the economy of his hometown. He had done his fair share of work on a neighbor's farm throughout his young life and along with the disciplined running each morning had fashioned for him a physique that was catching the eye of every lovely young lady in town. Beyond his physical prowess, however, was Matthew's desire to use his intellect and talents in order to shape a career in the fine arts and business world after he returned from serving his country.

At a young age, Matthew realized he could sketch and draw anything that his mind had envisioned for him. Along with embracing a desire to utilize this wonderful talent he decided that after earning a degree in business from college once he returned from the war he would establish his own advertising agency.

The day Matthew left for boot camp at Plattsburgh on the other side of the state of New York bypassed in sadness anything he had encountered in his life to that point. Hugging his father and mother good-bye only started the emotions flowing.

For the only time in her life, Holly was put on a leash. Matthew had tried to walk away from the house twice but Holly only followed him. Once restrained from going with Matthew, she sat there and let out sad whimpers. Matthew came back for one last pet good-bye and knelt down to touch her. Holly jumped to her hind legs and placed each paw on Matthew's shoulders in an affectionate embrace that his parents, overcome with emotion, could no longer witness.

Matthew returned home eight months later to the unrestrained excitement of Holly. Upon seeing her boy, now a man hardened and scarred by war, but always her boy in her heart, Holly whinnied and squeaked and whimpered in such elation as she rolled at his feet and jumped to his shoulders to lick his face to celebrate their reunion that Matthew feared her having a cardiac reaction before calming down.

Her golden fur paws tugged at his shoulders as he knelt down to exchange his emotions with her, but it was a one-sided exchange. Matthew wanted to hug Holly so bad, but the stubs on each arm stopped at his elbows. An embrace of any kind was impossible. In between Holly's excited moves of rolling around his feet, jumping back up on her hind legs, and wrapping her paws on Matthew's shoulders reaching around his neck, the most Matthew could do was rub his face against the soft fur of her side amidst a flurry of licks and kisses that for the first time since he lost his arms in the Battle of Cantigny brought smiles to his face and laughter into his life.

The overwhelming emotions he experienced at the reunion were short lived. Despite being awarded a medal for bravery for saving the life of another soldier when he picked up the German potato masher grenade that landed between them and throwing it away from them, his mind never let him embrace his heroics that saved the life of another young man. Shortly after his spontaneous act of self-preservation, German machine gun bullets shredded both of his hands and forearms as he attempted to move forward with the rest of his platoon after exiting their trench. Twelve of the men with him were killed instantly, if not simultaneously, due to the ferocity of the German fire which seemed to be concentrated wholly upon the point of their attack. His arms were so mangled and so much blood covered his body that at first those surveying the aftermath of the battle thought Matthew was dead.

During his convalescence in a field hospital and then a medical facility in England for a few weeks, the only thought Matthew dwelled upon was how his life was useless. There was nothing an armless artist could do to draw or sketch the imaginary and creative ideas which used to fill his head. The depression he sunk into destroyed that creative impulse. He quit talking to his doctors and nurses. He ate sparingly and lost a lot of weight, though no one seemed to notice. Everyone focused on his armless stubs when they first saw him, or so he thought that's what everyone focused on. He had no desire to run and the feel of the air against his face as he and Holly would take off at what he called a sprinter's pace for a long distance early morning run that had been a daily part of his prewar youth would never be experienced by either of them again.

Being with Holly was exhilarating for the moments that were the initial reunion, but within a few hours of being home Matthew had sunk back into a state of depression. The only thing he offered up to his parents was that his heart felt empty. They weren't sure what he meant by that but he didn't explain and they quit inquiring when he just stared at them expressionless. Holly seemed to understand that something had changed as well. She sat next to him during the day as he sat in an antique chair in his bedroom and like the old days of their youth she jumped up on the bed next to him at night in an attempt to snuggle as close to him as possible and help keep him warm. Not only could he not pull the blankets up around his shoulders as he lay there each night, but he couldn't wrap his stubs around Holly to hold her tight against him either.

Within a month of being home Matthew died. Holly tried in vain to wake him up that morning with her regular barrage of face licks but to no avail. When Matthew's parents came into his room to bring Matthew his breakfast that morning Holly was laying with half her body across his chest and her face tucked into the crevice of Matthew's neck. She let out a soft whimper when she saw them enter the room. Never did a golden retriever look as sad and lost as Holly did that morning.

As the glorious warm rays of sunshine shot forth from the clear blue sky adding another layer of warmth and love to the overall scenario taking place, the attention of Saint Francis of Assisi was diverted to Matthew and Holly, one of endless master and pet reunions taking place throughout the Garden of Eternal Friendship. The intensity of the emotions they displayed for one another was a living definition of happiness. It was as though neither wanted to be the one who quit first showing how much they savored the moment. The scene was so overwhelming that Saint Francis had to wipe away a few tears from his own eyes with the back sleeve of his dark brown robe.

"Let me give you a break," Saint Francis said as he reached down to rub Holly on the stomach. Lying on her back, her jowls seemed to loosely jiggle a bit as she enjoyed the continual tummy rub. Her tail wagged back and forth endlessly in a show of satisfaction and contentment in being with her human again.

"Thank you very much," Matthew said as he began to massage his own hands. "I didn't know how to stop, not that I wanted to, but

I have to admit that my hands were getting a little tired." He paused, and then spoke with solemnity in his voice. "How can I ever thank the Lord enough for having my hands back? I missed so much the sense of touch, to feel the softness of her fur, and the warmth of her body, to be able to embrace her again with the same unconditional love that she offers up to me."

Saint Francis smiled in approval at Matthew's comments of gratitude as well as Holly's continued enjoyment of the tummy rub. "The Lord already knows how you feel, Matthew. I can assure you He is most pleased by your thoughts for you have shown an appreciation for His kind works here in His house."

"I can't wait to draw again," Matthew remarked in a most respectful tone. "I think I have a lot of lost time to make up for when it comes to using my gifts. With Holly at my side, I am looking forward to that very much."

St. Francis smiled in approval. Holly finally rolled over and now stood on all fours. She rested her head on Matthew's lap.

"Any ideas about what you intend to draw first?"

Matthew momentarily closed his eyes and smiled all the while his left hand gently rubbing Holly's head. "I think I'll draw a portrait of Holly and myself finishing up one of our runs together. Our faces will show satisfaction and contentment, that we are happy to be our old selves again. I think my mom and dad will like that."

50

Erich Mueller was another of those looking for a person who they didn't know but had through fate and the confusion of war came in contact with long enough to form an emotional bond. Early in the war he was doing reconnaissance of the enemy positions. After crawling across No Man's Land in the pitch of night, he had managed to slip between some coils of barbed wire and from a slightly elevated niche of ground he was able to peer into the trench of his enemy. In the bottom of the trench they had the slightest of fires burning, the source of energy maybe no more than three or four slats of wood from an ammunition cart in a feeble attempt to warm their hands. Erich and his friends had done the same thing on numerous occasions. He thought it interesting how soldiers in both armies were willing to disobey orders of no fires in order to feel a few moments of warmth on the tips of their fingers or the palms of their hands. Occasionally, when the single flame flickered, it partially illuminated the face of the Scot who seemed to be doing the most talking. Erich couldn't make out what any of them were saying but the tone of their conversation led him to believe the topic was more personal than war related. When the Scot laughed and a smile broke across his face, Erich thought how much the enemy soldier looked a little like his younger brother.

In the skies above a star shell illuminated the heavens and cast its deathly glow over the battlefield. It was soon followed by the echo of distant machine gun fire but within moments the sounds of war were buzzing in Erich's own ears. Somewhere in the darkness behind him he heard the groan of some anonymous figure reacting to being hit by a bullet or maybe a piece of shrapnel. Shells soon began to land in the vicinity where he was lying motionless. His nerves kicked into overdrive and the perspiration of fear soon absorbed into his uniform making it stick to his skin. Another shell landed close enough next to him to make his ears ring, but he knew in his situation the best way to handle the maturing events was to lay still and endure and hope that luck was on his side.

The Scots he had been watching appeared to regard the evolving actions as nothing but a nuisance for they remained huddled around their flame. As Erich continued to observe them he found himself admiring their sense of calm. Then in a flash they were gone. The shell that landed in their trench rained down upon Erich large amounts of soil and rocks which he felt thump him in the back and ting off his helmet. After unclenching his eyelids, he scanned the trench where the Scots had been. Dust and smoke was still obscuring his vision as well as the darkness. The fire the Scots had huddled around was gone.

Numerous star shells now dotted the sky and in between flickers of light Erich caught glimpses of his opposite numbers. The bodies of two of the Scots were against the back wall of their trench showing no motion of life. The third Scot, the one who had reminded him of his brother, was no fewer than ten feet away from him. The blast had thrown his body into the air. His legs were dangling in the trench while his arms and torso were stretched over the rim and into the first few feet of No Man's Land. He was bleeding from numerous wounds to his face and neck but from what Erich could gauge, he was still alive. He could hear him groan, make a feeble attempt to clear his throat and spit, and then gasp for air.

Hearing enemy voices from somewhere in the trench below kept a steady flow of fear coursing through Erich and paralyzed his desire to move in any direction lest he give himself away. The wounded Scot continued his dying in slow steps while Erich watched and listened. Erich winced in empathy of the man's pain. The sound of a new shell exploding was a welcome moment of silence from hearing the dying man's agony.

Erich felt impotent. Continued fear for his own safety precluded him from any physical movement or attempt to provide comfort to the suffering Scot. Even if he did, there was nothing he could do to save him. So he began to pray.

"Holy Mary, mother of God, pray for us sinners, now at the hour of our death, Amen. Holy Mary, mother of God, pray for us sinners, now at the house of our death, Amen."

He knew it wasn't the whole "Hail Mary" he had been taught in those long-ago days of childhood, but he repeated the closing line of the prayer over and over again for close to quarter of an hour. Eventually, no longer hearing any sign of life coming from the direction of the suffering Scot, and with exchange of gunfire between the two sides fading for the night, Erich cautiously inched his way backward in order to extricate himself from the barbed wire coils and turn around to begin the long crawl back to his own lines.

Walking around in heaven for a few hours, unable to find who he was looking for, Erich had just sat down on a bench overlooking a small pond. In a little bit of frustration he mumbled louder than he realized, "I'm never going to find him up here, I'm never going to find him up here."

The young man passing by at just that exact moment stopped dead in his tracks and turned toward Erich. Each of them glanced at one another in little more than a casual way.

"I recognize that voice," the lad said with the touch of a Scottish accent to his words.

"And I recognize that face of yours," said Erich. "Though I didn't get to see all of it that night I saw you by the fire in the trench, I know it's you."

They showed similar smiles of discovery and joy and shook hands with the commonality of lifelong friends.

"My name is Archibald Cruickshank," the Scot, Erich's long-lost suffering Scot, began. "Call me Archie, as is the habit of my pals."

Archie had quit shaking but Erich held onto his hand. "I'm confused, Archie. I never talked to you. I never—"

Archie put his free hand around Erich's shoulder. "I heard you praying for me that night. I couldn't talk any, the blood in my throat was choking me, and as I lay there knowing that I was dying I could hear your soft, rhythmic tone over and over. Holy Mary, Mother of God, pray for us sinners, now and at the hour of our death, Amen. They were comforting words in my last moments of life."

Erich was close to losing control of his emotions and he rubbed his eyes clear. "I'm sorry I couldn't do more that night for you, Archie. I was too scared to move out of concern for my own safety. I prayed for years after that night that God forgive me for my selfishness."

"Look where we are at. I believe he listened to you," Archie said with self-assuredness in his tone. "I think he always listens to us when we ask for the right things in our lives."

51

The child held on tight to the hands of his mother and father as they walked toward another of the vast feasting halls where so many continued to gather and celebrate. He had been born in Holland and when his parents moved to live with a family member in France in June 1914 just outside of Paris, he was as excited as any seven-year-old would be for a new adventure in a new country. The stories his parents had read to him at nighttime before tucking him into bed for a good night's slumber had sparked in his young imagination places of great adventure and magic and he believed as only a young lad could that he would soon experience those in his new country.

Sadly, they had only been living in their new house in the countryside a few months when the armies of the western powers first clashed in the struggle of one side to conquer Paris and the other side to save it from captivity and destruction. Artillery shells had killed his parents. There had been so many hundreds of thousands of shells flying back and forth that it became impossible to discern who was responsible for the death of his parents, innocent civilians who only wanted, that particular day, to take their young boy on a picnic to the nearby stream where they might spend time fishing and swimming. The only thing that was sure was that before noon that late summer day he was made an orphan.

His plight didn't last long, though. A young French soldier had entered what was left of his house shortly after it had been partially demolished. It would have been impossible to gauge who was more scared at that moment, young Otto, who could barely see amidst the constant tears that were obscuring his vision amid the smoke from the burning embers and the death of his parents, or the teen age soldier Jerome Richard, who had been ordered by his senior officer to investigate the house and make sure it was clear of enemy soldiers who had been reported in the area. A smoking pile of debris that had once been a peaceful domicile, made a perfect place of concealment for a sniper with a scoped rifle.

Jerome was sweating and shaking so uncontrollably from fear as he entered through the broken front door of the kitchen that he was almost on the verge of fainting. He strained to keep his eyelids open instead of wiping them free of droplets of perspiration for fear of momentarily blinding his vision.

In the end it didn't matter.

Jerome fired his rifle into the partially destroyed room from which he heard a noise emit. There was no return fire in his direction but that didn't quell his fears. He tossed a hand grenade into the room to comfort his nerves. He was so unsure what to do after it left his hands that when it exploded he was still partially standing and pieces of debris from the explosion splattered against his uniform, though hitting him with nothing serious enough to cause him any physical wounds.

Knowing his commanding officer would want to know if the house was void of any enemy, he inched his way forward into the room that still hung with smoke from the explosion he had caused. He didn't have to go into the room the whole way before he could see the small lifeless body of Otto lying on the floor. Blood was leaking forth from one of the ears of the seven-year-old.

Jerome slumped to the floor in the doorway between the two rooms. He was so overcome with grief that when he tried to scream in anger and disgust at what he had done his vocal cords failed him. He sat there for more than a quarter of an hour staring at the boy whose life he had ended with such extreme, indiscriminate violence.

His mind was scrambled in a state of distress. This wasn't what war was supposed to be like. How was he supposed to reconcile what he had just done? How could he explain it to his parents when he returned home after the war? If this was what happened during his initial combat experience, how much worse was it going to get once he encountered real soldiers? Was there anything worse he could experience than killing a child? How was it fair that he was alive and a young innocent was killed in his own house? The questions raced through Jerome's fragile peace of mind and his body began to shudder as though he had a bad case of the chills. When he opened his mouth this time words of anger came forth in a froth of rage.

He continued exorcising his demons while cursing himself as he placed the tip of the barrel of his rifle under his chin and flailed with his fingers for the trigger. It didn't take long before his index finger hooked around the curved piece of metal and pulled it back, setting in motion the bullet that drove through his mouth and exited the back of his head along with fragments of blood, bone, and brains.

Jerome recognized Otto when he caught a glimpse of him turning his head toward one of his parents as they proceeded toward the Sea of Galilee Dining Hall. The feeling in his conscience and soul verified that it was the boy he had killed that day. Jerome raced toward the trio and soon found himself standing in front of them. It was then he realized that he had nothing prepared to say to them.

Otto solved Jerome's dilemma by releasing his grip from each of his parent's hands and then stepping forward to wrap his arms around Jerome's waist. His parents knew who Jerome was. The wetness in Jerome's eyes told them all they needed to hear from him.

"It was an accident," Otto's father said in a tone to help comfort Jerome. "You have nothing to apologize for," he added. "Otto told us what happened that day."

Otto's mother put her arm around Jerome who was overcome with emotions. "We've already prayed for your soul. We're sorry you did what you did to yourself. What happened to Otto was a misfortune of war that couldn't be avoided. When we entered heaven this morning we asked God to forgive you for your actions during the war, they were influenced by events no young boy from any nation should have had to experience."

Jerome could only whisper a soft "thank you."

"Will you come eat with us?" Otto asked Jerome as innocently as one would expect from a seven-year-old.

Jerome smiled and nodded in approval. He reached down to grab Otto's outstretched hand. They entered The Sea of Galilee Dining Hall and looked for a place to sit.

52

Vera Brittain had never imagined in all of her postwar years of loneliness and disillusionment what the great reunion with her dearest friends in the whole world would be like. She was excited for them when they made the decision to fight for God, King, and Country and supported them every step along the way as they embarked on the adventure of their lifetime. She never envisioned that by the end of the war she would be the sole survivor of their unique clique, left to face life alone until her own death in 1970. Vera spent the remaining years of her life pondering what life might have been like had it not been for the so-called Great War.

As the war survived from year to year it claimed her dear friends one at a time. Her heart ached in anguish when news reached home that Victor Richardson and Geoffrey Thurlow no longer shared a place among the living. Her plans for a future with her fiancé Roland Leighton were shattered when he died of battle wounds shortly before Christmas. The light of her life, her dear brother Edward, almost came back to her but fate claimed his life in June 1918. It was extra painful to see how close he came to making it back alive, but there was no comfort in knowing that he died late in the war since it made no difference for when the war ended he wasn't coming home.

She tried in the postwar years to accept what happened in the war. Her book, *Testament of Youth*, allowed her to keep the memories of her friends alive. Those who read of her memories and emotional scars could find some solace in knowing that their pain was being experienced and shared by others of that generation who would always consider themselves to be lost, cheated from a life of normalcy, not to mention the shattering of their belief in the humanity of mankind.

Vera and her cherished friends embraced with a passion that defined their love for each other. The depth of their friendship in the younger days of their lives, before the war destroyed all that was glorious and sacred and beautiful to them, was rekindled the instant they wrapped their arms around one another and felt the warmth of their emotions rejuvenating their spirit of life. The smiles that flashed between them were contagious to everyone who witnessed their reunion. Perhaps their reunion symbolized the rekindling of the faith and love that had lain dormant in the millions who survived but had no idea how to deal with the immense void in their lives in the postwar world.

That void was now filled as the Grand Reunion continued in all of its richness.

53

The elderly gentleman strolled through the mass of individuals who had gathered in St. Luke's Viewing Park without paying much attention to them, though as he passed them he found great pleasure in seeing so many people laughing and smiling as they enjoyed their own personal reunions. Jens Legrand was only nine years old when the Germans had invaded Belgium. Living in Liege he experienced the mighty barrages of the German seventeen-inch howitzers which blasted private homes and public buildings to piles of rubble. Like many civilians caught up in the advancing armies which constituted Germany's Schlieffen plan, his life was altered by the violence that fell upon his small country.

A short distance from his home which had miraculously gone unscathed despite the continual shelling, Jens was out in the street collecting the discarded refuse souvenirs of war. Empty shell casings of all calibers, from rifle to mortar shells, littered the ground. He didn't know why he was attracted to them, it was just something he found himself doing, perhaps the curiosity that makes a child a child getting the best of him.

He never heard them coming, they were just there, a multitude of apparitions that appeared to originate out of thin air. Large numbers of German soldiers walking through the streets of his town. Their demeanor was nonchalant. They strode with an air of supremacy about them, as though they had already won the war. On most, their guns dangled from shoulder straps and bounced against their bodies as they walked. A few of them carried their rifles in the strong clench of a tough hand wrapped around the midpoint of the stock while the other hand brought swigs of relief to their mouth from canteens filled with cool, refreshing water. Jens watched them unafraid as they got closer to where he was standing.

He waved at them with his right hand in a simple gesture of friendship while reaching into his oversized pants pocket where he had stockpiled the debris of war he had been busily collecting. Jens wanted to share with the soldiers his finds of the day. Feeling among the slivers of shrapnel and the smaller round bullet casings, his fingers wrapped around the larger round object and he pulled it out just as a trio of German soldiers stopped in front of him.

Their smiles evolved into emotions of fear as they recognized that the hand grenade Jens was offering toward them in the palm of his hand did not have a safety pin in it. The safety feature had snagged on the rough patch of linen that was the rim of the pants pocket and unknown to Jens he had five seconds to live. Two of the German soldiers turned away from Jens as they dove to the ground in hopes of limiting the danger the blast was going to do to them.

The third soldier dropped his canteen, pushed Jens in the chest with such force that the lightweight boy flew backward a good five feet before falling on his back, and dove on top of the grenade in order to absorb its explosive impact. The muffled crump of the grenade going off was what Jens would remember most about the foreign soldier who was a complete stranger to him, saving his life that day. He tried to look at his savior's face but his comrades upon checking him to see if he was still alive rolled their friend back over and he lay in the dirt face down. From underneath of him Jens could see a dark red liquid seeping forth and pooling about a foot from the deceased.

Walking through heaven Jens knew that eventually he would find the young man who changed his life that day. His faith in God that had guided him the rest of his natural life, the final sixty two years as a priest, was solid. As Father Nathanael, the name he chose upon committing his life to the works of the Lord, he had made a special pledge to himself the day he took his vows, to help those in need unconditionally and without question, just as the unknown soldier from an invading nation had done for him, allowing him to live and prosper, and give back to the Lord.

Their eyes met when they were still a fair distance apart and their simultaneous smiles verified that each was who the other one was looking for at that moment. They embraced when they met even before exchanging words with one another.

"My name is Kurt Becker, Father."

"I'm Father Nathanael, my son. I've been waiting a lifetime to thank you for saving me that day. Because of you I dedicated my life to God. Because of you I've been able to help thousands of people throughout their lives. Why did you do that?"

Kurt shrugged his shoulders, a little overwhelmed at hearing that he had such an impact on Father Nathanael and the lives of so many others. "When I first saw you, you reminded me of my younger brother. I had got news earlier that day that he had died in an accident back home on our farm. Maybe I wasn't thinking clearly when I did what I did but when I saw you with that hand grenade I just knew I couldn't let anything happen to you. Maybe by saving you I thought I could do something good and my brother's death might not have been in vain."

Father Nathanael was in awe. "I am sure God's reward for you in heaven will continue to be great. Have you been reunited with your brother prior to our meeting?"

"No, Father. Meeting you was my first priority. I wanted to make sure that you were here. I wanted to find out what happened to you. I am comforted by learning that what I did during the war had a positive impact. Many of my generation have come here believing that their lives were a total waste. I know that heaven will grant all of us a second chance and here we will be able to make the most of our gifts and talents, but it is rewarding in its own way knowing that in the span of my short life on earth, I did at least one thing that had a positive impact on the life of another."

Father Nathanael paused a moment to consider the views expressed by the young man.

"Many times the impacts of our actions cannot be understood. God does work in mysterious ways and that will always be something that confounds us as humans, even now as we reside in his house. But I do know and I can assure you that each life has something positive to offer for the benefit of others. It is during our most trying times that we must have faith in God's plan for us, especially during those moments and events we least comprehend. As long as you have faith in God and love Him, you will enjoy eternal life."

54

The children of Halifax, Nova Scotia, were together again. It wasn't just a reunion of childhood friends but one of family and community members as well. The war had intruded into their lives one clear, cold December morning in 1917. As the townspeople went about their daily lives, eating breakfast, preparing to send off their children to school, settling into the first hours of a day-long shift in one of the local businesses, two ships carrying cargo for the war effort ran into one another in the harbor. The *Imo* carrying coal and the *Mont-Blanc* carrying tons of TNT, picric acid, fuel, and guncotton were the catalysts of the ensuing explosion that resulted from their unfortunate collision. It was estimated that only the nuclear explosion that would be unleashed in a future world calamity would surpass the violence and force of the detonation that would emit temperatures over eight thousand degrees.

Within seconds the power of the blast destroyed every building in town. The human toll of 1,952 killed included close to five hundred children. Thousands more of all ages were wounded or scorched from the intense heat and fires that resulted from the catastrophe. No one had ever believed that so many people on the home front so far from the fighting taking place across the Atlantic Ocean would ever be lost for any reason during the course of the war.

The people of a whole town reuniting in heaven were without parallel, but they created some of the most impressive and lasting images of The Grand Reunion.

Albert Hook, his wife Violet, and their six children looked like two entangled octopuses as they group hugged, the gaggle of eight sets of arms pulling them closer and closer as they laughed, smiled, and cried, unable to restrain their emotions as the moment overwhelmed them.

Vincent Coleman and his wife Frances bounced their one-year-old daughter, Eileen, in their arms. Their older children, Eleanor, age seven, Gerald, who was eleven, and Juanita, one year a teenager, took turns hugging and kissing their baby sister as well.

One of the more touching scenes was that of Julia Carroll and her six-year-old daughter Lily, meeting their man for the first time since the explosion. Husband/Daddy John was off fighting in Europe at the time of the disaster and by the time he got back to Halifax months later his beloved wife and child were already buried, as were the nearly two thousand others. Making matters worse at the time was the fact that their home was totally wiped out as well, and any physical reminders that John might have been able to hold in his hands as an enduring way of maintaining some sort of connection with his family no longer existed either. A small black and white photo of Julia and Lily that he carried with him in Europe was the only picture of them that he possessed. Over the time up until his own death years later, he had looked at it and touched it so many times that it was ragged and the photo itself faded. The years after the Halifax explosion were only filled with sadness, loneliness, and despair.

Unlike soldiers in combat who prepare ahead of time for combat situations, the people of Halifax had no inkling of what was going to happen to them that particular morning. When the explosion occurred, no one knew what had happened, and many had been killed due to the initial blast. Of those who survived, they spent the rest of their lives trying to comprehend how so many loved ones, family members, friends, and neighbors could just disappear in less than the blink of an eye. Of the many bodies discovered in the wreckage of the manmade disaster, scores could not be identified due to the disfigurement caused by the blast and resulting fires that consumed persons and property.

In God's House, they were whole again, just as they were before the blast. They arrived at the pearly gates en masse, just as they had departed their lives on earth. Those who died that day due to the explosion found their family members and loved ones who had lived the rest of their lives in mourning and sadness lining one of the entrance roads into heaven. At first, overcome with a miasma of feelings, their emotions paralyzed their movements. It was too much to behold seeing everyone together again. A momentary staid look of amazement apparent on so many faces morphed into teary-eyed smiles followed by heartfelt cheers and furious clapping. As the distance between the groups was eclipsed, their legs carried them into the arms of one another in a celebration of love most of them hadn't felt since that December in 1917.

Understanding the numbers that would constitute those involved with this particular reunion of souls, The Heart of Divine Life Dining Hall was reserved specifically for those from Halifax. It was one of the larger dining halls in heaven and the acoustics for music were top notch. However, at times during the week-long revelry that came to be known as the "Halifax Reunion" the sounds of laughter and joy of those reuniting with their loved ones was louder than the music being played by the multiple bands which provided the dancing rhythms.

55

His last hours were occupied by the deceased body which lay a short distance from him while he himself lay dying on the battlefield. Occasionally a bite of pain distracted his thoughts from the faceless body that garnered his attention more than the stomach wound that was seeping his own life away. He was only twenty-one years of age himself and knew his earthly life would conclude sometime that day. He had come to accept his fate in an oddly comforting way.

He felt his identity disc dangling from around his sweat-caked neck. He checked his pay book and journal to make sure that his name was legible and not smeared over with blood. At least after he passed he knew that when he was found, those in charge of disposing his body would be able to record who he was and let his parents know. He shifted his vision to the unidentifiable mass of flesh that began to offer up to his senses a rather unsavory aroma.

He couldn't tell whether the deceased was friend or foe, not that it mattered anymore. The fact was he could barely discern that the charred body part had once been a human being. The skull was caved in. The poor soul's hair had been burned off as was the skin of his face all the way down to his chest. His legs were bare except for his skivvies which covered his privates, affording the deceased the only shred of decency possible in an otherwise wretched and vile scenario.

James's eyes did a quick recon of the area but came up empty in locating the missing pants. They were nowhere within his eyesight. It was just another inexplicable result of war. At this point in his life, his last lingering hours, nothing made any sense. Despite that quick realization, James continued to stare at the destroyed face. Slowly, just as slowly as he was dying, James began to wonder what the fellow a few feet from him used to look like.

Was he young like him, someone who was blinded by patriotic enthusiasm instilled in them by their misguided elders, or was he an old timer, someone who had been in the military for years and believed he could protect the young lads on the battlefield till the end of the war and bring them back home to their mothers?

Was he handsome in a rugged way, like a hero, or was he child-ish in his appearance, like James knew he looked like through the eyes of everyone else but himself?

What color was his hair? Was it dark brown or jet black? Or maybe it was bright blonde like the sun or sandy-colored like that of his own. It was probably short, James reasoned, like all the new soldiers who had got their first military regulation haircuts just a short time ago. It was hard to believe the war had started just a few months ago, and he had only been at the front less than seven days. He chuckled to himself knowing that others hadn't even lasted a full week like he had. For a fleeting moment he appreciated the extra time being alive that others hadn't been lucky enough to experience.

He gave the deceased body another viewing. Where a mouth used to be, James could make out a couple of teeth but the jaw line seemed to have been crushed in by something of massive force. He wondered whether the soldier who seemed to have suffered so much in a short period of time had one of those smiles that made the girls stop in their tracks and swoon, or did he carry a tight lipped look of seriousness about him? I guess it would depend on whether he was a private or an officer. James laughed to himself and quietly mur-mured, "Officers never smiled."

A jolt of pain shot through the left side of his neck. James gur-gled and tried to spit out some of the blood that was gathering in his throat. His weakness prevented him from doing so and he continued to choke to death in his own mixture of blood, saliva, and spittle. With the last effort of his life, though he could barely move any parts of his body at this point, James raised his hand a mere few inches and garnered enough strength to make a sign of the cross in the direction of the desecrated body of the unidentifiable soldier. "Hope to see you at the reunion," his lips gently whispered as his own life expired.

They met in heaven at the corner of St. Frances Xavier Cabrini and St. Rita of Cascia, the Patron Saints of Impossible Causes. James reasoned that that was the most logical place to seek out the identity of the soldier who had occupied his last thoughts while dying on the fields of France. He was a little apprehensive at how long it might take to locate someone he knew nothing about. He didn't know his nationality nor could he identify any specific facial features that might help in recognizing him among the humanity which was moving about. However, like everyone else was learning, heaven was not like earth, and nothing was impossible.

James knew as soon as they made eye contact each of them had found who they were seeking. They smiled at one another and their hands clasped in friendship.

It was satisfying to see what his unknown comrade in arms looked like before the war mutilated and desecrated God's greatest gift of life.

"I'm James," he said happily as their grasp tightened.

"I'm Friedrich," his new friend said overcome with giddiness. Their handshake evolved into a hug.

Friedrich was his own age. He could empathize with him in understanding what it was like to have his life cut short. They were the same height. Friedrich had short golden blond hair and a smile and facial features that would make a young lady enjoy staring into his soft blue eyes all evening. It was a shame man's ingenuity had designed mortar shells and land mines and other weapons of comparable ilk to erase such beauty from the world. It was an ugly use of wisdom and the mind.

They sat down on one of the black and white marble benches a little way back from all of the foot traffic along the major pathway and chatted as one would expect friends to do.

"I can't explain it even now, but as my body lay there, already physically dead, I could still feel your presence that short distance from me. Maybe it was my soul still in the process of exiting my remains, but I could feel your concern for me."

James shyly lowered his head. "I was thinking how my parents and family would feel if I experienced the same fate as you. At least they were able to identify me and give me a proper burial with a headstone for my loved ones to visit. It's still there at the Brandhoek Military Cemetery in Belgium for my great grandchildren to call on."

"My marker is also in Belgium. It is on top of a mass grave of unknowns who shared the same unfortunate experience during the war."

Friedrich paused to rein in his emotions.

"I wanted to thank you for the blessing you gave me."

James shrugged sheepishly.

"I did not think it was proper for you to die alone, though I know it was all too common an occurrence. You are quite welcome."

"I would like you to meet my family later," Friedrich offered up. "I want them to meet my friend who while his life was ebbing away took time to show me compassion. I would be honored if you would join me and my wife and children later for a meal at the great dining hall."

"I was about to ask the same of you my friend," James replied with satisfaction.

56

They were moving up to the front lines. It was exciting. His adrenaline was pumping. It was the highlight of his fifteen years of life. Because of his size he had been able to lie his way into the United States Marine Corps at the local recruiting station back home in Kentucky. Years of working in the coal fields alongside his father had allowed James Arthur Nelson's body to become accustomed to the rigors of a strenuous life. Before he was ten he was in the mines pulling and pushing tubs filled with coal along the narrow paths from where the coal was being collected to the carts being filled for extraction to the surface. At times he would be harnessed to the tub filled with coal as he lunged forward pulling and straining to carry out the job which helped supplement his father's pay and allowed them to continue their life of drudgery living in a company town in the hills of Kentucky.

Compared to his life before the war, boot camp was a breeze. He had actually enjoyed the physical training and it had made his features more solid. Fourteen new pounds of muscle bulked up his nearly six-foot frame. On the rifle range he ranked number four in the whole 5th Marine Regiment. Becoming a soldier was just another part of his life which had denied him the pleasures of being a child.

His unit was preparing to jump off into the fighting in what was referred to as the Aisne-Marne sector, a short distance from the town of Chateau Thierry on the Marne River. It would be his first combat experience. It would be his last combat experience as well.

Incoming machine gun fire from the German positions began to shred members of his regiment catching them exposed in large numbers in a wheat field as they approached the outskirts of the lovely old town. Somebody in command had made a grievous error.

The mind of the young ex-coal miner had a hard time comprehending everything he was witnessing. Yards ahead of him he saw the men on point buckle to the ground as their bodies twisted and contorted in a myriad of ways suggesting they had been hit by a deadly crossfire from well-concealed German gunners. James swiveled his head to the left in time to see his sergeant get killed. It was inconceivable how a human face could be shattered to a pulp in three seconds. James could hear tiny bony fragments from the sergeant's face ting off his steel helmet as he dropped to the ground in a futile attempt to find refuge in the flat open field.

Fear entered him. It reminded him he was only fifteen years old. His body began to shake. A body fell on top of him. It was another dead Marine who died with blood freely flowing from the dozen and a half machine gun bullets which holed his body. James became disoriented. He pushed the lifeless body to his side and tried to run away to safety. It's what a child does when he is scared and has no inhibitions.

James made it two steps before the bullets began to stitch his body in a pattern that suggested more than one gunner had him in their sights. A hole opened in his thigh. Two bullets hit the back of his hand which was grasping the stock of his rifle as he attempted to run. A fourth projectile hit his forearm, breaking the radial bone. His bicep and triceps were torn apart. More bullets broke his clavicle and his right arm dangled.

On the left side of his body bullets pounded into his chest though one rose slightly higher and pierced his neck. James could hear himself gurgle. As his mouth opened emitting sounds of anguish, another bullet entered it and blew out the cheek on the right side of his face.

Pain surged throughout his body from all of the damage inflicted in less time than it takes a person to sneeze.

Death was working fast on James.

He whimpered.

"Mommy, please, Mommy. I just want to be your little Jimmy again."

Death silenced him.

He died that day in the wheat field lying on his back, eyes wide open staring toward the heaven in which he now found himself seeking his mother who he had called for with his last earthly breathes.

As James passed through the gates of God's House on this grand day, his mother was there waiting for him, as was his father. Neither were images of their harsh life on earth. They were in their prime, as was he, as prime in life as a six-year-old could be. Jimmy's wasn't the only life reshaped to allow the wonders and pleasures of childhood to be experienced again, especially one that had been denied during a mortal existence. The reality was that it was more common than anyone realized, if anyone happened to be keeping track of such events, but there was no need for that in heaven. Here, life, in all of its stages, wonders, and joys was everlasting.

It was a simple mystery unraveled to those granted access to the celestial residence of the Creator but remains incomprehensible to those who have not yet been called home—heaven is whatever one wants it to be.

57

They were four among many of the dreamers and visionaries who saw their talents maligned by the war. Where once they envisioned using words to illuminate the mysteries of life and the beauty of society, in praise of all that is good in humans and the wonders that constitute God's world, they found their idealism severely questioned and punished by the visions of hatred and deprivation that war laid upon them.

After only a few weeks at the front, his spirit depressed by the realities of war, seeing the flower of youth killed in such huge quantities, Alan Seeger foretold his own mortality with his poem, "I Have a Rendezvous with Death."

> *I Have a rendezvous with Death*
> *At some disputed barricade,*
> *When Spring comes back with rustling shade*
> *And apple-blossoms fill the air-*
> *I have a rendezvous with Death*
> *When Spring brings back blue days and fair.*
>
> *It may be he shall take my hand*
> *And lead me into his dark land*
> *And close my eyes and quench my breath-*
> *It may be I shall pass him still.*
> *I have a rendezvous with Death*
> *On some scarred slope of a battered hill,*

When Spring comes round again this year
And the first meadow-flowers appear.

God knows 'twere better to be deep
Pillowed in silk and scented down,
Where love throbs out in blissful sleep,
Pulse nigh to pulse, and breath to breath,
Where hushed awakenings are dear...
But I've a rendezvous with Death
At midnight in some flaming town,
When Spring trips north again this year,
And I to my pledged word am true,
I shall not fail that rendezvous.

Disenchanted more and more with army life and its absurdities witnessed firsthand, Siegfried Sassoon expressed his disillusionment with the human spirit in "Attack."

At dawn the ridge emerges massed and dun
In the wild purple of the glow'ring sun,
Smouldering through spouts of drifting smoke that shroud
The menacing scarred slope; and, one by one,
Tanks creep and topple forward to the wire.
The barrage roars and lifts. Then, clumsily bowed
With bombs and guns and shovels and battle-gear,
Men jostle and climb to, meet the bristling fire.
Lines of grey, muttering faces, masked with fear,
They leave their trenches, going over the top,
While time ticks blank and busy on their wrists,
And hope, with furtive eyes and grappling firsts,
Flounders in mud. O Jesus, make it stop!

Imbued with a strong sense of nationalism and a commitment to the cause, Lieutenant Colonel John McCrae of the Canadian Army penned perhaps the most famous of The Great War poems when he wrote shortly before his exit from the land of the living in 1918 "In Flanders Fields."

> *In Flanders Fields the poppies blow*
> *Between the crosses row on row,*
> *That mark our place; and in the sky*
> *The larks, still bravely singing, fly*
> *Scarce heard amid the guns below.*
>
> *We are the Dead. Short days ago*
> *We lived, felt dawn, saw sunset glow,*
> *Loved and were loved, and now we lie*
> *In Flanders Fields.*
>
> *Take up our quarrel with the foe:*
> *To you from failing hands we throw*
> *The torch; be yours to hold it high.*
> *If ye break faith with us who die*
> *We shall not sleep, though poppies grow*
> *In Flanders Fields.*

Perhaps the most chilling indictment of the war came from the beautiful mind of Wilfred Owen, another exceptional talent destroyed by man's incessant inhumanity to man in the waning days of the war. His thoughts painted a sorrowful picture of the existence experienced by those condemned to live at the front as they waited to meet their fate.

> *"Dulce et Decorum est"*
>
> *Bent double, like old beggars under sacks,*
> *Knock-kneed, coughing like hags, we cursed through sludge,*
> *Till on the haunting flares we turned our backs*
> *And towards our distant rest began to trudge.*
> *Men marched asleep. Many had lost their boots*
> *But limped on, blood-shod. All went lame; all blind;*

Drunk with fatigue; deaf even to the hoots
Of tired, outstripped Five-Nines that dropped behind.
Gas! Gas! Quick, boys! – An ecstacy of fumbling,
Fitting the clumsy helmets just in time;
But someone still was yelling out and stumbling,
And flound'ring like a man in fire or lime…
Dim, through the misty panes and thick green light,
As under a green sea, I saw him drowning.
In all my dreams, before my helpless sight,
He plunges at me, guttering, choking, drowning.
If in some smothering dreams you too could pace
Behind the wagon that we flung him in,
And watch the white eyes writhing in his face,
His hanging face, like a devil's sick of sin;
If you could hear, at every jolt, the blood
Come gargling from the froth corrupted lungs,
Obscene as cancer, bitter as the cud
Of vile, incurable sores on innocent tongues,
My friend, you would not tell with such high zest
To children ardent for some desperate glory,
The old Lie; Dulce et Decorum est
Pro Patri mori.

(It is sweet and right to die for your country).

They met in heaven earlier in the day perhaps not by coincidence running into one another in the Garden of Eden. Here was the longed-for utopia where many of the idealists, poets, and intellectuals were congregating. They basked in the soothing warmth of the sun's touch while sitting about at leisure in plush green pastures as they put God's gift to them to use, each of them finding contentment in being able to write about a new world, one of generous life, infinite beauty, and eternal love.

Alan Seeger sat on the lush green grass with his back against the base of the giant oak, his legs stretched out before him. On the pad in his hands the words seemed to flow.

He wrote:

"I Have a Rendezvous with Love"

I Have a rendezvous with Love
At some majestic site
When Summer's pleasure shines upon us God's grace
And wild flowers fill the air—
I have a rendezvous with Love
When Summer brings us days of comfort and care.

It may be she shall take my hand
And lead me into her bright land
And open my eyes and take away my breath-
It may be I shall hold her hand, and to her wed.
I have a rendezvous with Love
On some satin sheets of shared bed,
When Summer comes round again this year
And the first golden sunflowers appear.

God knows the passion I keep
For the vision I see of purity and in white gown,
Intertwined in security of blissful sleep,
Side by side, feeling her breath touch my cheek,
Where gentle intimate moments are dear . . .
I have a rendezvous with Love
From dawn to dusk, each glorious morn and sensual night,
And I to my heart and thy wife am true,
I will honor that eternal rendezvous.

Lolling around in heaven, it didn't take long for Siegfried Sassoon to be reinvigorated with the desire to write. The tone he set in his new works distinctly different from his wartime poetry. His first creation in heaven was an instant favorite and requests for copies could not be run off by the head printer, Brother Dominic, fast enough to meet the initial demand.

"Celebrate"

The triumph of life has begun
Since the early morn, we celebrate the glory of God and his Son.
Raucous, joyous, unbridled the emotions flow,
Feel the warmth, the security of being home where all are one.
Children frolic about amid laughter, all is gay
It is the feeling of family, where no one is alone.
With games and toys and fine foods and joyful drink,
All will remember and cherish our new first day.
Lines of cheery, smiling faces, saved from death's brink.
They laugh and love, emotions going over the top,
While time means nothing for God's glory will never stop.

John McCrae hadn't stopped grinning since walking into heaven a short time ago. The freshness of life maintained a wonderful tingling throughout his body. He had already witnessed Seeger and Sassoon pouring forth their thoughts and once he found a suitable spot to sit and collect his own thoughts he began writing as well. His hand moved with a flourish as he penned a new classic.

"In Heaven's Fields"

In Heaven's Fields the roses grow
Between the lavender row on row,
They mark our place; and in the sky
The larks, sweetly singing, fly
Happily heard amid the love below.

We are now the living. A few generations ago
We suffered, felt pain, saw the sunset of life laid low,
Now we love, and are loved, and we toast life
In Heaven's Fields.

Enjoy the celebration with our brothers
All you who join hands with beloved fathers and mothers

The Holy Spirit; be yours to hold it high
Here with our Faith returned, with loved ones who once died
Never again shall we sleep, but rather enjoy here where the roses grow
In Heaven's Fields.

Wilfred Owen had enjoyed the past few hours chatting with other poets who like him were overwhelmed by the images they had witnessed since being welcomed home by Saint Peter. Even as he spoke with friends he had not seen in such a long time, his mind was spinning with the language he would use to describe what he saw before him. As the population of those he shared salutations with waned, he found himself a quiet solitary spot under the embracing branches of a vast weeping willow. Joy and contentment filled his spirit. He was so excited to put thoughts to paper again that he had to catch his breath. Then he began to write. The words flowed forth like water cascading over a steep precipice.

Dulce est domus Dei, in (It is sweet to live in God's House)(Sweet is the house of God)

Unending smiles, as happy children on Christmas morn,
Arms flailing about, cheering like fanatics, we praise the day,
Amid the glorious hosannas of angels, our new life is born
Festive are the moments for days of suffering and death are done away.
Too long we have been asleep. Those who had lost their younger years
those we laid in their graves, those who went lame; and blind;
rejoice today in ways that make life grand; gone is the grasp of fear.
God has welcomed us. His love is endless, all powerful and kind.
Life! Life! Shout it loud everyone! An ecstasy of delight,
Echoes of joy never again to be cast aside or denied;
Blinded no more by ignorant hate, only images of love fill our sight,
Void of those who ignited a not so Great War, callous leaders who lied.
Bright, across vibrant landscapes and skies of ecclesiastic rapture,
All, one family, one people, how much I enjoy them celebrating
In all my dreams darkened by despair, never a vision I thought I'd capture,
All one family, one people, how much I enjoy them celebrating.

If in some magical way another generation could be in this place
As one of those who have been aglow in the light since being left in
And see the eyes of eternal life lit up as is the smile on each loving face
How quick they would shake war free from their grip, the devil's sin.
If they could fathom at every crisis the images of everlasting love
Breathing forth from strong, healthy uncorrupted lungs
Innocent as a new born, pure as God's symbol, the dove
Perhaps wisdom would pour forth from their tongues.
Maybe then they would say,
As I can attest to with great pride
It is sweet to live in the house of the Lord.

58

The crowds were enormous leading up to as well as inside of the Saint Vincent de Paul Dining Hall. The honoree was a humble individual who was so overwhelmed upon hearing that the festivities would be held in his honor that he had spent a morning earlier in the week in a special meeting with God the Father respectfully asking that it not be held. He did not feel comfortable in being singled out or praised above others for his actions on Earth.

The banner which stretched across the front wall of the hall, with gold-plated letters six feet high, however, summed up what God the Father had told Herbert Hoover in their private get together.

WHOEVER IS GENEROUS TO THE POOR LENDS TO THE LORD, AND HE WILL REPAY HIM FOR HIS DEED. (Proverbs 19:17)

Early in the war as Belgium came under control of the German armies and the British blockade of Europe went into effect, the non-combatants of the tiny country began to experience the pangs and eventually the death grip of starvation. Heading up the Commission for Relief in Belgium, Hoover and his organization eventually helped to send over five million tons of food to the people of the war-torn country, who in 1914 had only wanted to stay neutral. Hoover spent countless hours throughout the war appealing to the good nature of individuals as well as governments in helping to raise money in order to procure foodstuffs to save a nation of suffering souls.

The enormous task of shipping the food across an Atlantic Ocean infested with U-Boats, warships from all nations as well as thousands of indiscriminate floating sea mines, and then distributing it to the people of Belgium throughout over two thousand villages, cities, and towns continued as long as the war lasted.

Despite criticism from governments actively engaged in the war who claimed that the act of charity in order to aide a suffering human-ity was actually benefiting opposing belligerents, Hoover put every waking hour of his life into the operation. Famine and malnutrition was an enemy who attacked without feelings of nationalism guiding their actions. They destroyed the most vulnerable of innocent babies and children as well as the fragile and aged who warring political entities seemed to forget about or worse, ignored in the midst of war.

After the war Hoover continued in administering food relief operations through organizations under his coordination to millions of people in central Europe, Germany, and Russia.

Long lines of people who once stood outside of relief stations throughout Belgium and numerous other war-ravaged nations on a daily basis waiting for life-sustaining sustenance now stood inside and outside of the St. Vincent de Paul Dining Hall waiting for Hoover to appear. The murmuring sounds of hundreds of thousands engaged in their private conversations were soon overwhelmed by the astounding blasts from thousands of trumpets blaring out the opening chords of "Handel's Hallelujah Chorus."

As Hoover appeared the people began cheering and clapping. The adulation embarrassed him, one could tell by the pink to red blushing that overcame his face. Overwhelmed by such an out-pouring of emotion for himself, he eventually let a smile slip forth from his otherwise solemn demeanor. Seeing his sheepish grin only encouraged the people to increase in volume their appreciation for all he had done on their behalf during the darkest of times.

Hoover's actions proved that humanity can rise above warfare if one makes the decision and puts forth the determination to do so. He had no idea that so many of the people he strode past and waved to in acknowledgement on his way to the steps leading into the hall had survived the war and its chaotic aftermath and gone on to live full and productive lives because of his unselfish efforts on their behalf.

Jesus and His Father met Hoover and his wife at the doors of the great hall. The quartet exchanged embraces and Hoover turned around to face the crowd that had closed in behind him. He was so choked up with emotion that when he tried to speak he couldn't vocalize any of his thoughts. Jesus stepped forward to lend a hand. As he placed his arm around Hoover, Hoover dabbed his eyes dry with the part of the white robe that draped over the shoulder of God's only Son.

The last chords of Handel's masterpiece faded, and the people sensing that Jesus was about to speak to them quickly quieted.

"In a time of great evil and upheaval, our brother lived by the words of the great commandment, 'Love one another as I have loved you.' He gave of himself for the benefit of all people. He is now beyond righteous, as of this moment forever after, being anointed by me through the power of my Father into the Sainthood of his Kingdom."

A half hour later when the uproar of the appreciative throngs had finally settled, Hoover stepped forward, his composure having been regained, and with the utmost of respect in his tone and demeanor, offered up his thoughts.

"I was guided by the belief that what really matters is not what one said, but by what one did. I thank you, God, for this honor, and I pledge to uphold my responsibility as a saint. In a life that sometimes is all too short, I was blessed with a long one, and I am truly happy in knowing that along the way I was able to do something good for the sake of so many other people. I haven't met my parents up here yet, but when I do I hope they tell me they are proud of me."

When the cheers of appreciation finally faded after his short remarks, Hoover and the multitudes proceeded into Saint Vincent de Paul Dining Hall to enjoy a feast for the ages. Food, sustenance that for so many of them had been something they had ached for over long periods of time, was now available to all in abundance without limitation. However, gluttony was nowhere to be found. In the land of milk and honey, no one would be in want.

Hoover sat down with his wife and shared some warm, fresh-from-the-oven bread rolls which brought one's taste buds alive without the need to slather butter or any topping on it for that matter, with two young children who had made their way through a sea of adult legs so they could sit across the table from the recently appointed saint. As Hoover made eye contact with the most precious of God's Kingdom, even though their names were yet a mystery to him, he surmised that they had once been war orphans, or at the least victims in some way of the war.

He reached across the table to shake their hands.

"Please call me Herbert," he said in a jovial tone.

"I am Anna," said the six-year-old girl.

"I am Raphael," said her brother, who was but one year older than his lovely sibling.

Hoover slid a plate of fresh strawberries and whipped cream in the direction of his new friends. They reciprocated in kindness as Raphael held a cup in the air as Anna filled it with steaming hot coffee. Once it was filled to the brim he gently placed it on the ivory white china saucer without spilling a drip or a drop.

"Thank you, so very kind of each of you. Your parents should be proud of your manners and kindness."

Hoover watched as they both experienced the coolness of the cream on top of the strawberries making contact with their mouths. The sweetness brought their taste buds alive as they hadn't been in over a hundred years.

"Is it as you remember," he gently inquired.

There was a moment before they responded. They were savoring a taste of life that had long ago been taken from them.

"During the last weeks of our lives all we had to eat was grass in boiled water," Anna stated in a matter of fact way.

"We had run out of real food in a quick way," Raphael piped in. "For a while everyone talked about the war, but soon everyone only talked about food because there wasn't any to eat. Mother said the soldiers took it because they needed their strength to fight."

Hoover quit sipping his coffee but he continued to hold the cup in his hand rather than place it on the saucer. He was transfixed by the story the children were telling him. They spoke as the innocents they were. There was no motive behind their words, it was just what they remembered most about their short childhood days before the war had come and slowly taken their lives from them.

"I don't remember what fruit tasted like," Anna said. "I do know these strawberries are the tastiest treats I have ever eaten." A smile followed her declaration as she stuck her fork into another of the rich, red seeded fruits peeking out from underneath a second layer of fluffy whipped cream Raphael had plopped on top of the original dollop while Anna was talking to Hoover.

Raphael grabbed the largest berry off the plate with his fingers. Somehow he fit the whole thing in his mouth, save some of the extra cream which remained around the rim of his lips.

"Mother wouldn't like you not minding your manners," his little sister gently scolded him.

Hoover smiled.

Raphael rolled his eyes but still offered up an apology at the same time licking the whipped cream from his face and fingertips.

"I don't blame you at all, young man," Hoover stated. "Wait till you taste these cherries," he said with pleasure in his voice as he slowly moved a bowl full of them in their direction. "Just let me know if you want whipped cream on these as well."

59

Alleluia!
I love the Lord because He has heard my voice in supplication,
because He has inclined His ear to me the day I called.
The cords of death encompassed me;
the snares of the nether world seized upon me.
I fell into distress and sorrow,
and I called upon the name of the Lord,
"O Lord, save my life!"
Graciousness is the Lord and just,
yes, our God is merciful.
The Lord keeps the little ones;
I was brought low, and He saved me.
Return, O my soul, to your tranquility,
for the Lord has been good to you.
For He has freed my soul from death,
my eyes from tears, my feet from stumbling.
I shall walk before the Lord
in the lands of the living. (Psalm 116)

Heaven had a way of allowing nationalistic inhibitions to fall away like the changing leaves of autumn. Throughout the vastness of the Saint Vincent de Paul Dining Hall, other meals of gratitude, thanksgiving, old as well as new friendships and joyousness were taking place. The overall scene was not just a coming together of families from nations which had gone off to war against one another, but they were gatherings of God's people who reveled in the sharing of those familial recipes and tastes which they had longed for so much while suffering through the despair of the battlefields or the physical debilitating hardships imposed by blockades or scorched earth policies implemented by the governments of the warring nations. Countless numbers of soldiers who had spent idle time in their trenches, dugouts, foxholes, or bunks waiting for the fighting to resume as The Great War played itself out day after endless day often wondered what it would be like to encounter their hated enemies and be able to see them as fellow humans (with few exceptions as those of the Christmas truce had done) were enjoying that wondrous moment of cordial enlightenment.

"It is beyond what you boys remember what it tasted like," Edward Middleton said softly as he closed his eyes while savoring the bite of roast beef. The caramelized onion gravy which complimented the juiciness of the oversized bite he shoved into his mouth only seemed to highlight flavors of the other seasonings which made his taste buds reach out for more. The black peppercorn, dried thyme, celery seeds, and perfect dash of olive oil complimented the freshness of the perfectly prepared meat.

Other members of the Pals battalion group which had met earlier in the day were relishing the moment they had talked about so many times waiting in the trenches in those days before they met their fate that first of July in 1916.

Kenneth Willington smiled in appreciation of the enjoyment his friends were experiencing as they sliced off portions of the roast beef and passed them around the table. He made sure, however, to only accept a small slice that would not interfere with the rather thrice-the-size cut he took from the platter of roast lamb. Prepared in gravy made of white wine and lamb stock, he could taste the delicacy in his mind before he even let his lips wrap around the piece making its way toward his mouth courtesy of his knife and fork. Upon completion of that small movement his body seemed to find comfort in once again enjoying the fanciful recipe from his youth. The garlic and rosemary from the lamb mixed with the delight of the aforementioned gravy combination to, dare I say it, create a taste of heaven.

The others razzed him and chuckled when Riley Alistar Kinkaid put aside his main course and focused first on dessert. "I've waited too long for this," he said with the innocence of the child he was that day his time on earth had come to a conclusion. "You can have your meats and meals but nothing will ever taste finer than some fresh apple cheesecake, or apple cake, or custard patties," he said as he reached for a Florentine made with blackberry jam. They laughed louder as Riley realized he had no extra room on his plate for the Florentine so he happily consumed it eliminating himself from any further conversation while he chewed and treated his palate to one his favorite childhood memories.

They were having the time of their new lives. No more would they know death of the senses of taste and smell. Never again would the odor of decaying unburied dead in the heat of a late summer afternoon clog up their nostrils forcing them to gag in a vain attempt to inhale a wisp of fresh air. Never again would the blandness of canned, cold bully beef and the challenge of chewing over cooked biscuits hard enough to chip their teeth interfere with them embracing the celebration of a meal with friends and family.

At a nearby table the Verhoven family shouted in glee at seeing the former German soldiers Johann Halder and Rudi Polder along with their parents making their way through the crowds to join them. It already seemed like ages since the young men had met with the Verhovens to apologize for their part during the war in executing Hugo's wife and children while he was being led away as a prisoner of war. What mattered at the moment was the surprise the Verhovens had waiting for their new friends, Rudi and Johann and their parents.

"Please! Sit! Join us!" Clara shouted with excitement as the children, Emil and Marga, pulled out chairs for their smiling guests.

They had barely seated themselves as the Verhovens began to place in front of them warm servings of Stoemp Aux Polreaux, Witlof with Ham, and fresh portions of molasses bread. "We know they may not be extravagant dishes, but it's the best we can do on short notice," kidded Hugo.

"I believe they are what the Americans would call 'comfort food,'" said Rudi as he inhaled the enticing aroma of the specially prepared potatoes.

"Nothing like we ever got at the front," chided Johann. They offered up first tastes to the Verhoven children but Emil politely declined.

"Father says that friends always get the first bite."

The warmth of the word "friends" coming from the young child only seemed to compliment the loving taste of the molasses bread which Rudi and Johann inhaled as they enjoyed the long-absent taste of their childhood favorites which they hadn't enjoyed since before they went off to war in 1914.

At the end of the same table involved in their own savoring reunion were Patricia and Ryan Benton and their mother and father. The young Britons who had died in the course of the war, Ryan at Messines and Patricia in an accident at the munitions plant where she had labored, had only met their parents a short while earlier in the most interesting of circumstances. As the siblings sat at the table taking a break from their unsuccessful endeavor of locating their parents, they were taken aback with great astonishment as their parents came toward them with hot meals in their hands.

Ryan Benton Sr. was carrying his son's favorite meal, Lancashire hotpot, while Catherine Benton placed in front of Patricia her preferred passion of the palate, Beef Wellington with wild mushroom Madeira sauce. It was a plate that she had sampled at a young age at a Christmas family get together and every time Patricia was able to relive that experience with a fresh course she had always joked to her parents that dining on such fancy cuisine put her on par with the royal family. While it wasn't very often they could prepare her the meal due to rationing of foodstuffs especially during the war, it was the meal her mom was preparing for her that day the messenger from the War Office had delivered the news about the accident at the munitions plant.

Ryan and Patricia had barely let their parents set the serving dishes on the table in front of them before they were on their feet wrapping their arms around their parents with unbridled emotion.

As much as the enticing aroma of the tender lamb and exquisite juicy beef wafted into their senses, it would be a long time before they let go of their respective embraces of their parents and they would sit down to enjoy their meal as a family as in days of yore.

Toward one of the kitchens of the great hall three individuals who were not bakers, nor chefs, nor for that matter had ever cooked anything in their lives, were busy preparing meals for those who they had slain in carrying out their obligations as snipers during the war. While Nikolai Yevgeny, Reinhard Kleist, and Nigel Chapman had come to understand the reason they were welcome into heaven after their earlier conversation with Jesus, they decided as a trio that they would continue to make peace with themselves by acts of service and kindness starting with those they had killed with their military prowess. Hundreds of those who they had made one-shot fatalities, along with their families who had suffered for years and decades grieving the loss of their sons and husbands at the hands of the three snipers, were also invited by the trinity to be their guests of honor this first day in heaven.

For hours the three of them brought out endless dishes and servings of celebratory pleasantries which included sweet honey-filled baked apples, simple but tasty raspberry Vatrushka buns, tantalizing slices of brandy and rum Prague cake, moist butter-laced Apfelkuchen German apple cake that sent taste buds into a tizzy of stimulation, and fresh-picked strawberry, blueberry, and blackberry custard whipped cream trifles topped with shaved chocolate that left no one satisfied with just one serving.

Reinhard paused as he placed the last portion of Prague cake from his tray onto the table. As he turned around to make his way back to the kitchen, his path was blocked by his own wife and two children. Though they had not seen him since before he had left to go fight in the war and his body was never recovered after he became a kill of an enemy soldier who mimicked his martial attributes, they had taken great satisfaction in seeing him serve those who occupied the tables before them. The wisdom of heaven had allowed them to understand what they were witnessing and they felt pride and adoration in the actions of their husband and father. Reinhard could see their love in their eyes and he smiled in turn at them. To describe the emotions he was feeling would challenge the talents of Shakespeare. It would take him time to regain autonomy of his heart strings and he would enjoy great lasting moments that day with his family. Afterward, however, Reinhard would go back to serving others, ensuring that they and their families would experience moments they would recall forever anytime they relived those first hours and days of their grand reunion.

It was that type of spirit which moved up the meeting between Douglas and Madison Stanton and their five-year-old son James with the former zeppelin commander Peter Strasser, who had led the wartime raid on their house which killed their son. At the conclusion of their initial meeting Madison had mentioned they would love to dine with the airmen but insisted that Strasser meet his own family first. Strasser, however, had been so touched by the act of forgiveness on the part of the Stantons that he wanted to share his first meal in heaven not just with his family at his side but with his new friends who had made him feel human again for the first time since being the perpetrator of such atrocities during the war.

Upon his death in 1918, Strasser, like many others who had initiated acts of warfare beyond those identified as recognized combatants, had experienced the uncertainty of purgatory which carried with it years of agonizing soul searching and the doubting fear that they would not be allowed entrance into heaven. Even after spending all the time he did seeking out and apologizing to his victims and his soul was cleansed by the forgiving grace of God, he remained in a state of emotional ecstasy for the gift of eternal life which had been bestowed upon him. It still tugged at his heart that his youngest victim had been an innocent five-year-old in the vessel of James Stanton.

Peter introduced the Stanton family to his wife, Katarina, and after seating each of them proceeded to serve them their meal as a sign of gratitude for their acceptance of him. "I hope no one minds but I wanted to try something new," Peter said in a matter of fact tone. "I was thinking this being heaven, we are going to have a chance to sample an endless variety of new tastes." Over steaming portions of fresh vegetables and garlic chive sautéed charbroiled steaks, with side dishes of dark beer battered freshwater trout and lemon rice pudding dessert, the two families spent time dining, laughing, and chatting getting to know one another as one would expect new friends to do.

Throughout the Saint Vincent de Paul Dining Hall the universality of food continued to contribute to the frivolity of the new good times. Freddie Stowers and his former Colonel P .L. Miles thought the best way to embrace their new friends of the former German army they had encountered and in some cases killed on the battlefields was to introduce them to some good old-fashioned South Carolina tastes and delicacies.

"There is nothing like Frogmore stew and some peach cobbler to guarantee to make you gentlemen smile," Freddie informed the gathering of one-time belligerents from the earthly world as they passed around some extra napkins to help those unaccustomed to the juiciness of the meal. Many of the young Germans had never tasted the invigorating flavors offered up by the mixture of sausage, shrimp, and crab combined with seasoned corn on the cob and baked potatoes slathered with butter and onions. "If you had enticed us with such delights in 1918, we would have quit fighting and brought enough cold lager for all of us," one of the young boys who had come from the Berlin region quipped, "and I can eat these Pimento cheese sandwiches every day of the week."

Similar scenes were playing out in the other dining facilities such as that taking place in the Sea of Galilee Dining Hall. Jerome Richard walked hand in hand with Otto, the young boy he accidentally killed while searching for snipers in domiciles thought to be abandoned. Neither of them had any intentions of eating anything other than sweets or desserts. "You pick one for me and I will choose one for you," Jerome decided. "That will make it more fun for each of us."

They soon stood in front of a glass case filled with a vast array of what appeared to be an unlimited choice of desserts one could ever have dreamed about. They walked slowly down the length of the case until Otto tugged on Jerome's sleeve and pointed his small index finger at the object of his sugar desire. "Let's eat that one," he said. "I've never had that one."

As Jerome perused Otto's pick, he told his young friend the same thing. "I've never had one of those either. Let's get one for each of us."

They sat at a table and studied their pick. It was a giant purple icing cream puff known as the Religieuse. A single serving was actually two tiers of pastry filled with vanilla cream. The flakiness of the crust was perfection, as if all the best mom bakers in the world had worked together to make this delight for the enjoyment of Jerome and Otto and the moment they shared. As for the vanilla cream . . . mmmmmm. But believe me when I say even six m's isn't enough to explain how good it tasted when your tongue and the roof of your mouth removed that piece from the fork and swirled all those flavors together. As one would expect, Jerome and Otto each had two of them.

Alleluia!
Praise the Lord, all you nations;
glorify Him, all you peoples!
For steadfast is His kindness toward us,
and the fidelity of the Lord endures forever. (Psalm 117)

60

It seemed as though only yesterday he was planting in place another of the circular land mines which would blow a person's leg off in a second of being tripped by some unsuspecting soldier. Like all jobs in the military during the war, it was a job that had to be done and someone had to do it. Danny hadn't been accurate enough on the rifle range to warrant the British Empire handing him a Lee Enfield so they taught him how to dig holes in the ground and set land mines in place.

The truth was he became an expert at it. In short time he could gauge the exact depth of the hole he needed to dig simply by doing some soil reconnaissance which was the simple process of probing the ground simultaneously with his middle and index fingers. They trained him to set in place mines that would blow up trucks or even artillery pieces being pulled by vehicles, though they never told him in basic training that horses pulling artillery pieces would also be maimed or killed when they set off the hidden explosive as well.

Once he was at the front lines, however, the only mines Danny saw were personnel mines that would maim or kill soldiers, usually one at a time. Once being assigned the job of mine layer, Danny thought he had been lucky in avoiding frontline combat, but he hadn't really thought out the scenarios that he would be associated with in being the demolition expert of underground ordinance.

While he would not be involved with any "going over the top" attacks which always ended in the useless loss of life, it would be his responsibility to bring to the front the land mines which he would plant in front of the trenches to further compliment the mass amounts of barbed wire which occupied the first yards of no man's land on both sides of the battlefield. This lonely endeavor took place at night when darkness would provide the cover needed for someone whose job placed them in front of the trench and not within the security of its walls and dugouts.

Digging at night and planting a mine at night led Danny to become an expert at doing things by feel. Never to risk the flash of a torch or even the flicker of a match flame, he had to gauge the deepness of the hole he laboriously dug with a hand shovel or sometimes his fingers as well as the width of it in order to evenly lay the mine in place before gently covering it with the dug-out soil. Another almost impossible challenge to overcome was to map where each of the mines he planted on a nightly basis were located so that his own soldiers would not venture into the newly laid minefield once they began exiting the trenches on their way toward the Germans lines.

On more than one occasion, Danny had witnessed the successful results of his specialty work when German soldiers trying to reconnoiter the British lines under the cover of the same darkness he relied on for his protection had crawled into a mine field previously set in place by his steady hand and cool demeanor. The results were as spectacular in their appearance as they were disgusting in their reality. Without notice an approaching enemy soldier would crawl over top of a planted mine and the pressure of the unwitting lad from someone's family back in Germany would set off an explosion that violated the sanctity of the quiet night. The pyrotechnics would illuminate the darkness in a spectacular display of orange flame and white, lightning-like flashes. Mixed in with the sound of the explosion would be the sharp cry of the life that was being extinguished in a quick second.

When daylight poked its face over the horizon the blown up and battered body of the would-be infiltrator would be seen by those in that vector of the trench who went about their duty with a feeling of satisfaction that Danny and the other sappers were doing their job in protecting them from night attacks by raiding parties. Because other mines that had not yet been detonated remained in place, no one was in any hurry to remove the deceased and so like many other dead that occupied so much of the battlefield between the trench lines, another nameless soldier, or what was left of him, rotted away throughout the day, food for the flies which swarmed in biblical hordes especially during the spring and summer months.

Danny was pleased with his handiwork because he knew he was helping to protect his pals and they appreciated him for that. He never gave much thought to those German soldiers who died as a result of his ever burgeoning expertise in laying mines until his worst fear was realized during another of the endless attacks by the men of his sector one July day in 1916.

The whistles from officers were sharp and shrill and they were easily heard the length of the trench. As they had countless times before, they signaled the start of another offensive that would end the war and they could all go home. From the security of a dugout he could see wave after wave of his brothers-in-arms ascend the ladders propped against the trench walls and make their way over the top toward the hated Huns.

Minutes went by and the belief that the attack was succeeding was quickly shattered by the numbers of British soldiers returning to the trenches they had exited to launch the attack. Danny came out of the dugout to reach up and assist a wounded soldier who had crawled back to the lip of the trench and then collapsed with just his hands hanging over the top of the ditch. Danny realized he knew the man. It was a sergeant who always needled him about making sure he didn't blow himself up while planting those mines out in the dead of night. Danny dragged the unconscious sergeant into the trench headfirst losing his footing as he did. He fell backward and landed hard six feet later at the bottom of the trench with the weight of the sergeant on top of him, pinning him long enough on the ground in a position which forced him to witness the scenario playing out a few feet to his left and above the trench.

Retreating soldiers fleeing the battlefield for the security of their trench weren't focused on the route they took to achieve their goal which resulted in a number of them running directly into the area where Danny had laid mines just a few short hours ago before the sun had come up. His brain registered the situation but all he could do while still burdened with the unconscious sergeant on top of him was yell a warning in the direction of the hapless soldiers who were seconds away from becoming casualties of his nocturnal handiwork.

The first man disappeared in a wave of smoke. Danny's eyes first saw the poor boy's boot hit a pitch of soil and then watched helplessly as the lad's body was propelled high into the air from the force of the detonation. Mixed with the visual ugliness was the horrid mangling of voices which emitted guttural sounds and sharp wavelengths of terror amidst the physical pain being wretched upon them. A second unfortunate saw his leg fly forth from his body and his brain registered the pain a second before his heart quit working. The next soldier made it a trio of casualties as he tripped over debris in front of the trench and fell forward, his chin hitting the ground with enough force to detonate another mine. His head tore off from his neck and came to a rest with his helmet still attached to it a few feet from where Danny remained helplessly laying, watching the results of his night's work.

A fourth Tommy was hit in the back with machine gun bullets from the Germans while simultaneously tripping off another land mine. His body contorted and shredded at the same time.

The futility of helplessness frustrated Danny and he closed his mouth as he observed the continuation of the unstoppable events. He could feel his head getting light and the rhythm of his heart slowing down. He didn't know why but he could feel his body emitting his fluids creating a damp warmness in his underwear and down the leg of his uniform pants. Another explosion from the mined area resulted in another body being projected through the air, this one landing on top of the detached head already occupying a portion of the bottom of the trench. The eyes on the new corpse remained open even though blood was seeping forth from both sockets. Despite the damage done to the deceased, Danny could make out that it was his friend William Nottingham. They had been friends since primary school days.

Danny could feel his stomach contract and then push its contents up his chest and out his mouth. It came with enough force that it created a geyser of nauseating chunks of blueberry muffins, crackers, and tea mixed with spittle and other indistinguishable body fluids which after they ended their ascent splattered off of Danny's face, some going in his nose and a little more back in his mouth, causing him to gag ferociously as he quickly turned his head sideways to try and spit out as much as he could.

More debris of war rained down on his private piece of trench including hot metal shrapnel which he could hear thud into the back of the sergeant still impeding his ability to escape.

Without any fanfare or signal, the noise of war came to a halt. Danny closed his eyes and whimpered in shame. The havoc and destruction due to his handiwork had never before been so prevalent.

Medics who soon arrived to proffer assistance instantly recognized Danny as being the only one still alive among the seven bodies and parts of bodies which surrounded Danny and his own personal war zone. As they pulled the dead sergeant off of him they could see the blood still running down Danny's leg. What he thought was his body urinating was blood from two pieces of shrapnel which had missed the sergeant and sliced into Danny's thigh and leg about three inches from his private area. Before they even placed him on the stretcher to carry him to the rear area to get medical attention, Danny drifted into unconsciousness from loss of blood.

A number of painful operations and seven months later, Danny's participation in The Great War officially ended when he was released from his military obligations due to "severe injuries suffered in the service to God and Country," so read the paperwork which made him a civilian once again. For months afterward, through self-imposed muteness as he internalized his wartime experiences and conversed daily with his maker in thoughtful prayer, Danny decided to offer up his remaining years and talents to glorifying God.

When he passed from his earthly body in 1992, family, friends, and community members would fondly remember Danny as the "Flower Man," the kind, gentle proprietor who brought so much beauty to the lives of others through the offerings that could be found in his local flower shop. Few were privy to the events Danny had suffered in the days of his youth, those days that were supposed to be the best times of his life.

As the soft, warm rays of heaven's sun comforted his muscles, Danny brushed back in place the rich, dark soil that surrounded the newly planted chrysanthemum. It was the last of three rows deep of interspersed white, pink, and yellow crysanths which was but a small part of the overall field of flowers row on row which greeted those heading toward the athletic fields which were located up and over the hillside.

Vibrant red and yellow canna mixed with Lily of the Valley gave off a romantic aroma of love which complimented the visual cornucopia of beauty. Colorado Columbine in their royal purple were present in such vast numbers they seemed to discredit the earthly world belief that these Rocky Mountain delights were ever rare in sight as well as quantity. They were offset by a sea of calla lily which was the essence of what we embrace when we apply the word "pretty."

As one would approach the apex of the hill they would be met by pink, yellow, and white lantana, the epitome of a graceful flower reinforced by the countless butterflies which flitted about them in their own aerial tapestry of delicacy. The lantana was one of Danny's favorites. He was always inspired by how the petal color would change as it aged. It was a reminder of his life and how he progressed from being a soldier of duty to a human of concerned empathy.

When asked later in life why he had such a dedication to raising flowers, Danny softly replied to the young inquisitor, "During my convalescence, I often dreamed what it would be like that rather than planting death in the ground I could spend my time seeding life, bringing endless moments of joy to people instead of being accountable for defiling a body of its God-given parts or blotting out a life in general." Perhaps subconsciously despite the lantana being Danny's favorite, he always seemed to plant more Blue Bells, that romantic favorite of nineteenth century poets that symbolized regret and solitude, in his garden displays.

Cresting the hill were Cherry Blossoms. In an atmosphere of endless spring, they would be perpetually in bloom, as would all of the others. Thriving dahlias and tulips highlighted sitting areas along the pathways. Roses of all shades, the rich red of love, the white rose in all its purity, pink and light hues of orange, and some of fresh, alluring shades of green were scattered in every direction.

This part of heaven was beyond words in trying to describe the beauty each person encountered.

Danny smiled as he thought about the majestic Oriental poppy plants that he would be planting tomorrow morning.

It was a feeling of serenity.

Danny was at peace with himself.

61

It was youthful exuberance taken to the extreme but that was nothing out of the ordinary for the two brothers whose personalities oozed overzealousness in anything that they did. From the time they were young to the time they went off to war and throughout the war itself they participated in the grand adventure of life with a zest that made others envious of their endless energy. They found excitement in everything they were involved with whether it was challenging one another to a long distance race just to see who could outrun the other or who possessed the superior hunting skills by being able to bag a wild boar or elk from the farthest distance.

Their childhood innocence remained part of their adult demeanor throughout their military service during The Great War. In a way it was as though the modern air war in which they found their martial calling had been designed especially for their entertainment. The joy of the hunt they had so often experienced in their adolescence accompanied them as they twisted through the clouds amidst the whizzing of bullets and the flaming of countless fabric-covered flying machines. They enjoyed basking in the glory and adulation which resulted from their ability to master the maneuvers which allowed them to destroy their enemies with unequaled proficiency.

It ended suddenly one early spring day when news reached Lothar that his beloved older brother, Manfred, had been shot down and killed by the combined ruthlessness of pursuing air power and antiaircraft fire from the ground. While his enemies would debate among themselves for decades who actually deserved the credit for the death of his brother, Lothar survived with the reality that the war had taken from him his spirit for life. His tears would fill more cups than he and Manfred would ever have emptied if they had been filled with wine, as they had been so many times during their celebratory sessions of brotherly enjoyment and revelry. The emptiness of not having his brother as part of his life gnawed at him all the remaining days of his own life.

None of those feelings of despair so happily dispensed to millions in mourning during the war years by Satan and his minions had any autonomy where members of The Grand Reunion were celebrating the joys of family and hearth.

When their eyes first met the shine of their smiles was blinding. Life surged through their veins as they embraced one another with hugs that initiated the wrestling match which others stopped to witness with great enthusiasm. Happy spectators moved back giving them room as they strenuously applied grappling holds on one another in their determination to be the first one to claim victory over the other in their initial competition in heaven. The shackles of darkness were absent, excoriated by their love of eternal life. They were together. They were having fun. They were the brothers of their youth again.

62

The pitch had never looked so pristine, certainly not like the patch of earth they shuffled around on in order to play a few matches during the Christmas truce that first year of the war. This time there were no shell holes pocketing the field that would host what was one of the most looked forward to events in the whole of the Grand Reunion. The debris of conflict did not litter the playing environment. The ground was not churned-up earth due to incessant shelling. The smell of death did not intrude upon the player's senses like it did that December so long ago. Perhaps best of all the air was not chilling to the bone or sharp to the lungs of those participating.

Everything was different this time.

The vibrant green grass shined forth a continual burst of color more than any artificial turf could ever hope to attain. The field being so perfectly groomed concealed no hidden holes or chunks of displaced earth that might inadvertently cause the ball to deviate from its projected path or result in a player twisting his ankle and suffering an injury that would prohibit further enjoyment of participating in the contest.

The sun was warm, not hot.

It was comfortable, with the slightest breeze gently wafting periodically the length of the field, enough to bring a soothing cooling off of overheated bodies which had become so in the throes of spirited competition.

They were all here, together again, as they had always said they would be when they met again, "in a better place."

Henry Scrutton of the Essex Regiment who had been one of the first Tommies to meet with the enemy in the open field between the trenches looked around excitedly for the young blonde-haired Bavarian he shook hands with that cold night. His name was Dieter Reimer. Henry had never forgotten it, or the feeling the two of them shared in learning they were both the same age and that both were students prior to the war with a shared interest in the study of biology. Until they met one another and conversed with one another that last magical Christmas of the war, neither had ever realized how alike they were.

Dieter's arms wrapped around his long lost friend's shoulder as he bear hugged him from behind.

"I just knew it was you, Henry," he said to him while the surprised but happy Briton managed to twist around to face his pal.

Their smiles said it all. After another embrace they took a step back and began chatting.

"I've waited a long time to return the favor," said Dieter as he reached into his pockets, retrieved a pack of cigarettes and slapped them into Henry's open palm. "That was the last time I had good tobacco," he said. "You made Christmas that night as memorable as any I've ever had."

Henry chuckled and from his pocket produced a small wrapped block of fresh sharp cheddar cheese and set it firmly in the palm of Dieter's hand. "It's not the same brand you gave me that night, but I promise you it's just as delicious."

Former members of other units and regiments from both armies shared similar reunions of friendship that had been established in the course of a few days amidst the circumstances created by the unofficial stoppage in the war that was the Christmas truce.

Northumberland Hussars, Argyll and Sutherland Highlanders and Royal Saxon soldiers in the youth of their earthly life reunited in these first days of their new heavenly life, the difference being their identity was no longer that of a militaristic organization but those of individuals of the human race as children of God in the presence of His house.

Albert Wynn and Johannes Niemann were among the others who now stood in the middle of the field still soaking in the beauty of the outdoor facility. During their match in 1914, Johannes scored one of the three goals the Germans scored to beat the Scots. This time it would be different since Albert and Johannes were on the same team. Here, there would be no division among nationalities since there no longer were distinct nationalities to be pitted against one another.

Those who had played in the 1914 matches were given the honor of playing in the first games in heaven. The St. Ignatius and Bartholomew soccer complex consisted of six separate fields. Enthusiastic, very vocal fans reclined on the gently sloped hillsides that enveloped each field.

From the second they began play, their bodies began to revel in the glory of God's design. Leg muscles began to stretch forward, arms pumped adding speed as one ran. Healthy lungs breathed in fresh air, hearts pumped with the excitement brought about by competition.

The smile on Albert's face as he dribbled the ball past a defender before sharply passing to Johannes who snapped a sharp kick that hit off the top corner post and out of play resonated with everyone.

Manfred Kindler, the goalie, understood as well as anybody what Albert's smile was saying. Manfred had lost his leg a few days after the Christmas truce during a bombardment when artillery fire was ordered to be used by those behind the lines to remind those in the front lines that the war was about killing each other and not making peace overtures or gestures of peace and goodwill to all men. His will to live shattered akin to his bodily wounds, Manfred died a few days after New Year's in 1915.

Though Manfred had missed the ball as it sailed high over his head on its way to banging off the metal post, the sheer thrill of feeling his legs beneath him as he shuffled from side to side positioning himself for the attempted shot would have been no less exciting had Johannes scored on his shot.

Bruce Bairnsfather watched the game from the hillside sitting side by side with Erich Erhlanger. They had parted ways back to their trenches the last day of the truce after shaking hands in a final gesture of common admiration and friendship, pledging that after the war they would meet on a regular basis and introduce their families to one another. Erich was killed the first day the truce ended by a sniper's bullet to the middle of his forehead. Bruce actually died before the truce officially ended when the pin of the Mills grenade he had strapped to his uniform snagged on to a piece of barbed wire and was pulled out just enough to set off the explosive charge. Most of his body was never found besides a chunk of his torso and fragments of his teeth and skull. Now they sat there in the prime of their life as their young children chased one another in wide circles around their respective dad and mom as the two couples enjoyed the game they were watching.

Back on the field as the game progressed Henry Williamson reveled in the feel of the physical contact between him and his opponents in athleticism. Hermann Hirschfelder and Ryan McGregor were double teaming him as he tried to dribble his way through them instead of around him. Their knees banged into one other each time Henry attempted to maneuver through them, intent on showing his adversaries that his physical prowess was enough to compensate for his lack of poetic movement that so many of the other footballers possessed and continually displayed throughout the course of the contest.

Just as Hermann dipped his foot forward to make the steal, Henry powered past him with a burst of speed that caught both Hermann and Ryan off guard just long enough for Henry to nudge the ball to the side of his kicking foot which allowed him to flick the ball flawlessly to his teammate running in full stride to his left. This time Albert Wynn faked a pass to Johannes Niemann and powered a shot that headed for the corner of the net. Albert was already throwing his arms up in celebration of a goal when his brain confirmed the vision his eyes witnessed in the goal crease. Manfred Kindler had originally slid to the side of the field that Johannes Niemann was progressing from as he anticipated that Albert would pass the ball to his teammate as he had done earlier in the game. Realizing just as quick that it was a fake and that Albert was the impetus behind the shot heading into the vacant part of the net, Manfred flung himself horizontally feet first into the air in what seemed like a vain attempt to stop what everyone watching believed would be nothing less than a sure goal. The bottom of Manfred's cleat hit Albert's kick from the side and diverted the path of the ball just enough to send it downward. The ball hit the turf with such authority that it bounced high enough in the air for Goodwyn Mathers, playing a spirited defense to the side of Manfred, to head it close to twenty-five yards down field.

The crowds were cheering in great appreciation of the jaw dropping skills being presented for their entertainment and enjoyment. Bruce and Erich alternated between hitting each other on the back and wildly flailing their arms in disbelief as they watched game play transpire in such quick bursts of action. But while they were applauding the chain of events previously described, their emotions were further enriched as the focus of the play on the field now quickly shifted to the other side of the pitch. The speed displayed by Jack Templeton, a teammate of Goodwyn Mathers as well as the recipient of his sensational header, stunned defenders who vainly tried to impede his advance to the promised land, defended by the last line of resistance, goalkeeper Tjaden Hinneman.

The thud from Jack's foot as he made final contact with his shot was loud enough to have fans divert their attention from watching a game on a neighboring field. The force was so powerful that even though Tjaden made contact with the ball with the gloved palm of his hand, the ball still continued on its path to the back of the net.

Those watching the game cheered and cheered and cheered louder and louder and louder.

Players from both teams who had not been involved with the play and had found themselves spectators on the field cheered just as heartily as those watching from the hillside. It was irrelevant who had scored or what it made the score of the game at that moment. Much like they had experienced that December night back in 1914 when they put aside their weapons of destruction in order to embrace humanity over hostility, they were celebrating their love of life and their love of the game and all of the athletic elements which defined the beauty of sports.

For those fleeting moments when they had decided to let their sense of humanity intrude on their sense of duty to country as espoused by misguided leaders who had encouraged them to embrace the belief that it was better to hate their fellow humans than to actually embrace them, those soldiers, those young men, had returned in spirit to the days of their childhood when all was ideal and it was in that all too short period of their lives when it was okay to love one another regardless of who they were.

Playing the game made them human again. It was something never comprehended by those who perpetrated and then protracted the war. Only Satan and his minions could have devised a system that rewarded those who killed their fellow man with medals and then deemed the acts heroic and extraordinary while punishing those who dared even for a few days to seek understanding and mutual respect with their fellow man.

Perhaps the greatest sin of the whole war was that those who suffered the most on behalf of their leaders found a solution to ending the war that first Christmas, that season of warm wishes and glad tidings, and those in power chose to look the other way not only allowing the slaughter to proceed unabated, but they continued to orchestrate it as well.

It was all the betrayed souls of the lost generation ever wanted, a chance to live a full life and enjoy the everyday joys of living.

In heaven life is eternal.

Even though he hadn't made an appearance on the field yet, rumor was Jesus himself had a devastating shot from the top of the box.

EPILOGUE

And I saw a great white throne, and Him that sat upon it, from whose face the earth and the heaven fled away; and there was found no place for them.

And I saw the dead, the great and the small, standing before the throne; and the books were opened: and another book was opened, which is the book of life: and the dead were judged out of the things which were written in the books according to their works. (The Book of Revelation, Chapter 21 Verses 11–12)

The Lord said, "Who in your opinion is that faithful, farsighted steward whom the master will set over his servants to dispense their ration of grain in season?"

That servant is fortunate whom his master finds busy when he returns.

Assuredly, his master will put him in charge of all his property.

But if the servants says to himself, my master is taking his time about coming, and begins to abuse the housemen and servant girls, to eat and drink and get drunk, that servant's master will come back on a day when he does not know. He will punish him severely and rank him among those undeserving of trust.

The slave who knew his master's wishes but did not prepare to fulfill them will get a severe beating, whereas the one who did not know them and who nonetheless deserved to be flogged will get off with fewer stripes.

When much has been given a man, much will be required of him. More will be asked of a man to whom more has been entrusted. (The Gospel of Luke, Chapter 12, Verses 42–48)

Not measuring anything in time as is the nature of heaven, it was difficult to decipher how long the Pearly Gates remained open until everyone from the World War I generation passed through to their eternal reward. Everyone, that is, except those who were denied entrance.

When the last of the deserving walked through the gates, they continued on their path without looking back. Saint Peter closed the last of the ledgers he carried in his hands and signaled to the gatekeepers to bring the gates together. They locked automatically upon touching and no human could pull them asunder.

Those left on the outside looking in stood in shocked, stunned silence.

Not only were they silent, but all was silent. No longer did the sound of trumpeting angels singing hosannas permeate the atmosphere. The last groups who had entered heaven before the closing of the gates were no longer in sight of those denied entrance. The apostles and saints who had greeted newcomers for endless hours turned and walked away. Those on the outside watched them diminish as they walked further and further away. Against the backdrop of a flat horizon, it took them quite a while until they were so far away that they couldn't be seen anymore.

For the entire time the group of outsiders remained silent. Some lowered their heads and scuffed at the stony ground with their shoes. Some quietly wept as they started to entertain the realization that they might not be getting in. Others who had remained proud and arrogant in life continued to maintain that same disposition as they waited for whatever was going to happen to happen.

Though no wind was blowing, the air seemed to grow cold.

God appeared before them.

There was no fanfare or any type of theatrics.

He began to speak.

The authority in His voice guaranteed that no one dare look away as he spoke, nor questioned his words.

"You were the leaders of great nations, leaders with great power in your hands, and you chose to waste that special gift.

"You embraced war and destruction, while shunning love and productive creativity.

"You let your judgment be blinded by selfish motives.

"You had it in your power to prevent war, yet you chose to perpetrate conflict.

"Your actions led to great multitudes suffering in pursuit of policies that benefited no one save your own personal greed and lust for power.

"Your wisdom was used to mislead those who looked to you for guidance, and you taught them to hate on behalf of empty nationalistic goals. Once you poisoned their minds you educated them with the methods to eliminate life. You manipulated the intelligence of the gifted into designing weapons of destruction not allowing them to pursue ideas beneficial to mankind.

"You used your ability to speak to deceive those who put faith in your words. You chose to teach hate one another instead of love one another.

"You rewarded those who carried out Satan's work, and imprisoned those who chose to speak on behalf of peace.

"In the end, you chose to kill instead of choosing not to kill."

None of those who were denied entrance could look God in the eye. All stood with their heads slanted down. None spoke in their own defense, not that it was possible to dispute God's words.

The moment of reckoning continued.

"You used your earthly wealth to create false images of yourselves, ignoring those who were in want.

"You denigrated life by establishing a culture of death.

"Once you started war, you had power to end it, but out of ego and vanity you justified its continuance.

"You had great resources at your service, and you chose to fashion them into weapons that led to humanity suffering in the vilest of ways.

"You cast aside the lives of millions in pursuit of your own selfish, worldly desires.

"Babies and children cried out for mercy, for food, for warmth, for love . . . and you ignored their suffering. You gave them starvation and disease. Your actions took their parents from them and left them orphans to die in the depths of despair.

"The beauty of the land fashioned for your enjoyment, and your care, you shredded with explosives and poisons. You brought forth pestilence and disease that bore sorrow and wailing into the hearts of those who placed their faith in you to do right by them.

"Your actions crushed the human spirit, bestowed upon each person by my hand. You made them doubt life and question my existence and love for them.

"You took all that was precious and beautiful in all that I gave you, and you cast it aside and destroyed it."

God paused.

"You are responsible for the suffering of this generation.

"Your guilt does not allow for your entrance at this time into my house."

God disappeared from their sight.

Their sight disappeared from their eyes.

They felt their health fade.

Soft skin turned rough.

Pimples and boils replaced light blemishes.

Fingers and toes curled outward until the bones snapped. They dangled, useless.

Fear exited their throats.

Aches crept into their bodies.

Their stomachs tightened and they began to wretch forth their contents.

The minions of darkness appeared unnoticed to carry out their work.

Unseen sudden blows broke the knees and ankles of each leg.

Their wailing of pain was heeded by none.

They lay in a field of stones in great agony.

Unable to rise, they tried to drag their broken bodies.

Broken fingers, knees, toes, and ankles offered no leverage.

Their identities were gone.

They were no longer monarchs, dynastic figureheads, parliamentarians.

They were no longer ministers, office holders, wielders of political power.

They were no longer selfish leaders of great nations and peoples.

They were no longer the decision makers of life and death over millions.

They were no longer the makers of widows, orphans, and lost family members.

They were no longer the possessors of great talent or obscene wealth.

They were useless bodies in great torment.

The minions of darkness gave them water but not enough to slake their thirst.

Squalid morsels were placed in their mouths to tease their hunger, not satisfy it.

Unable to move they existed where they lay.

They would remain in a state of suffering until it was decided otherwise.

On the other side of the Gates of Heaven, The Grand Reunion continued in all of its splendor and glory.

ABOUT THE AUTHOR

M. A. Kaye lives in the United States among the characters that inhabit God's gift of an imaginative and creative mind. It is hoped that *The Grand Reunion* is the first of many literary efforts which will bring enjoyment and entertainment to the reader for years to come.

CPSIA information can be obtained
at www.ICGtesting.com
Printed in the USA
BVOW05s0804261216
471811BV00002B/256/P